Vaastushastra

Vaastushastra

Vijaya Kumar

NEW DAWN PRESS, INC.
Chicago • Slough • New Delhi

NEW DAWN PRESS GROUP

Published by New Dawn Press Group
New Dawn Press, Inc., 244 South Randall Rd # 90, Elgin, IL 60123
e-mail: sales@newdawnpress.com

New Dawn Press, 2 Tintern Close, Slough, Berkshire, SL1-2TB, UK

New Dawn Press (An Imprint of Sterling Publishers (P) Ltd.)
A-59, Okhla Industrial Area, Phase-II, New Delhi-110020
e-mail: sales@sterlingpublishers.com
ghai@nde.vsnl.net.in

Vaastushastra
Copyright © 2004, New Dawn Press
ISBN 1 932705 04 X

All rights are reserved. No part of this publication may be reproduced, stored in a retrieval system or transmitted, in any form or by any means, mechanical, photocopying, recording or otherwise, without prior written permission of the original publisher.

NOTE FROM THE PUBLISHER

The author specifically disclaims any liability, loss or risk whatsoever, which is incurred or likely to be incurred, as a consequence of any direct or indirect use of information given in this book. The contents of this work are a personal interpretation of the subject by the author.

PRINTED IN INDIA

Contents

Preface	7
Introduction	9
1. Vaastushastra — An Overview	11
2. Basic Principles of Vaastushastra	13
3. Selection of Plots	19
4. Houses and Flats	36
5. Shops and Offices	71
6. Other Buildings	80
7. Landscaping	89
8. Vaastushastra and Feng Shui	93

Preface

This book is by no means an extensive study by a professional. The information provided in this book is my own interpretation of the subject, gleaned from various books, and presented from a lay person's viewpoint.

The book deals with various aspects of the subject, in a simple language, and serves as a ready reckoner for those who have no time to study the subject in depth.

The publishers and I hold no responsibility for any discrepancy in the script. We would welcome suggestions or intimation of errors that come to anybody's notice.

Introduction

Vaastushastra is an ancient science that deals with the observations of the law of nature and their effects on human life, in their dwellings. According to Vaastushastra, five elements – Earth, Fire, Water, Air and Sky – govern the principles of creation. These forces act for or against each other to create harmony and disharmony.

Based on the ancient Indian science of architecture, Vaastushastra pertains to the physical, psychological and spiritual order of the built environment, in consonance with the cosmic energies. It is a study of planetary influences on buildings and the people who live in them, and aims at providing guidelines for proper construction.

A house designed according to Vaastushastra creates a positive cosmic field to make your life smooth and happy.

It helps you match your biorhythms to the rhythms of the universe and respects your holistic relationship with nature.

Vaastushastra — An Overview

1. The word 'Vaastu' is derived from the root 'Vas', meaning 'reside'.
2. Vaastushastra deals with the architecture of designing and constructing buildings and assigning a proper place to each of the five basic elements.
3. A building constructed as per the principles of Vaastushastra will bring happiness, good health, wealth and prosperity to its inmates.
4. All matter and energy and all animate and inanimate objects in a building, have an interrelationship with each other and are connected by electromagnetic forces.
5. A harmonious and balanced combination of these electromagnetic waves result in peace, happiness and contentment.
6. In Vaastushastra, interacting energies are minimum in the north-east direction, which is therefore called the Direction of Heaven.

7. The south-west direction has intense energy stress, and hence is called the Direction of Hell.
8. Where buildings are not built according to Vaastushastra specifications, the deficiencies can be corrected by using symbols, colours, light and sound.
9. Rooms constructed according to the functional activities of the different parts of the body provide peace of mind and contentment.
10. Besides cosmology, Vaastushastra comprises astrology, physics, chemistry, various yogic disciplines and astronomy.
11. Asymmetry, helix and evolution play an important role in the science of Vaastushastra.

Basic Principles of Vaastushastra

1. The universe is a composition of five basic elements — air, earth, fire, space and water.

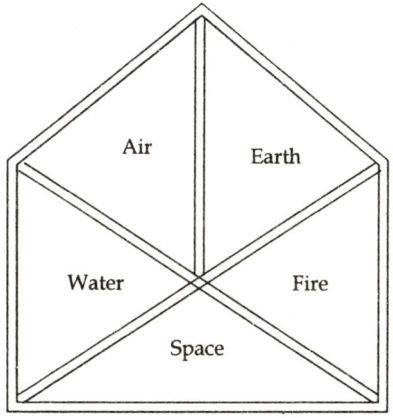

The Basic Elements

2. These elements sustain us by providing energy.
3. A dynamic balance of matter and energy, in relation to our body, gives more flexibility of body and mind, thus making life better and pleasant.

4. When there is disharmony between these elements, our energies dissipate and cause tension, stress, ill health, sorrow, depression, etc.
5. In order to maintain this dynamic balance of elements, we have to redirect our energies, subjectively and objectively, for happiness, success, wealth and prosperity, and quality life.
6. We receive internal energies in the form of proteins, carbohydrates, etc, and external energies in the form of heat, light, etc.

Elements	Sense Organs	Functions
Air	Skin	Feeling
Earth	Nose	Smell
Fire	Eyes	Sight
Space	Ears	Sound
Water	Tongue	Taste

7. The equilibrium of the elements on our planet is maintained forever. Water evaporates from lakes, rivers and other expanses of water into the atmosphere, where it accumulates as droplets to form clouds, and the sun's heat releases excess water in the form of rain.
8. Our mind and life should coexist with the five elements in such a way as to become the cause of our existence.

9. On emerging from the lifecycle, the life force merges into the cosmic force, thus becoming the cause.
10. This merger of these two forces is effected by meditation or detachment by which one rises above the elements.
11. The relationship of the energy centres in the body with the life force, mind and elements is shown diagrammatically here :

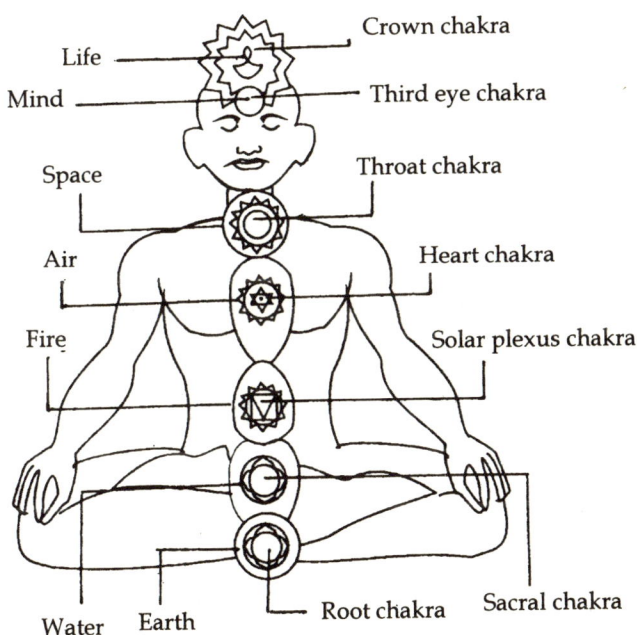

The Chakras

12. The elements should be assigned proper places during the construction of buildings.

a. The centre, assigned to space, should have the least activity.

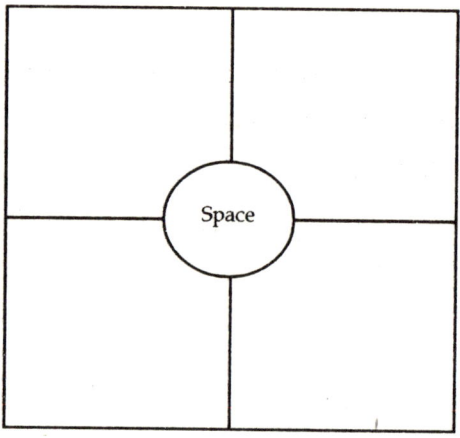

Space in the centre of the plot

b. The north-east, assigned to water, is ideal for water tanks, bore wells, swimming pools, etc.

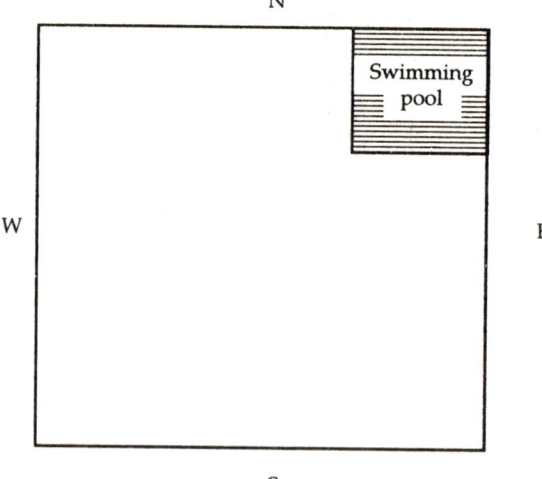

Swimming pool in the north-east

c. The north-west, allotted to air, would be suitable for a guest or as storeroom.

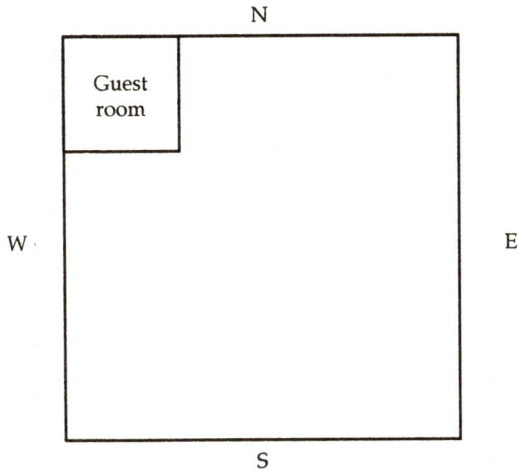

Guest room in the north-west

d. The south-west, assigned to earth, is the ideal place for most things, as earth is the most stable of the elements. Use this space as much as possible.

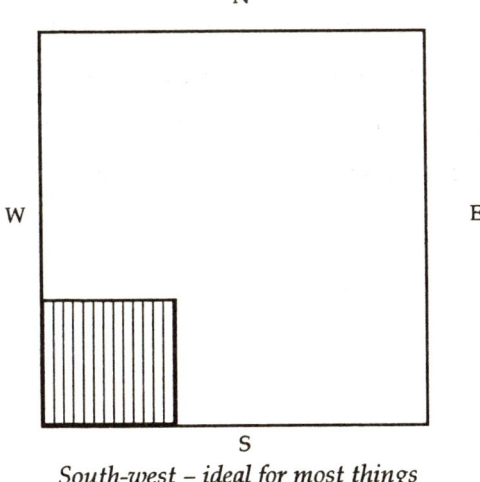

South-west – ideal for most things

e. The south-east, allotted to fire, can have the kitchen, boiler, furnace, etc.

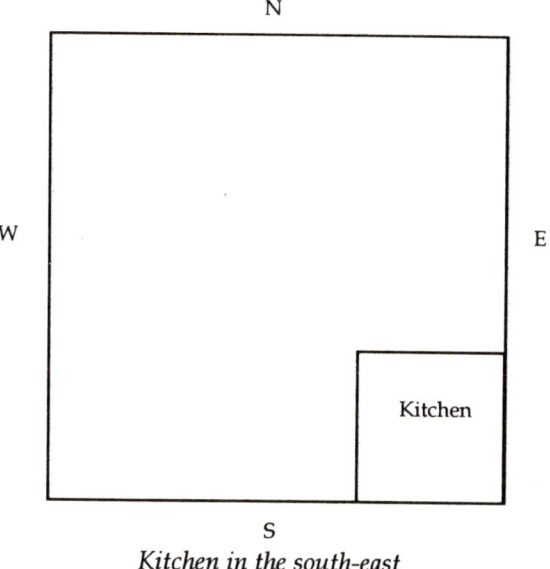

Kitchen in the south-east

13. An imbalance in these elements may manifest in the form of floods, earthquakes, volcanoes, etc.
14. Meditation helps in achieving and maintaining balance in the elements subjectively, by accelerating the process of energy flow.

Selection of Plots

Selection of plots, for houses, offices, factories, etc, is a vital principle of Vaastushastra. A good plot—well located, and facing the directions as per Vaastushastra principles—brings one happiness and good health.

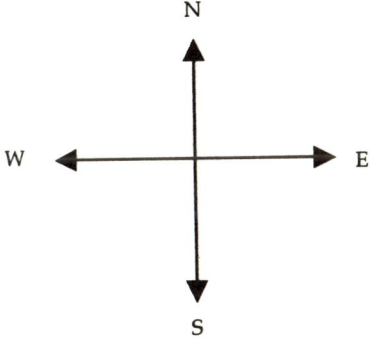

Directions play an important role in Vaastushastra

1. An east-facing plot is considered very good.

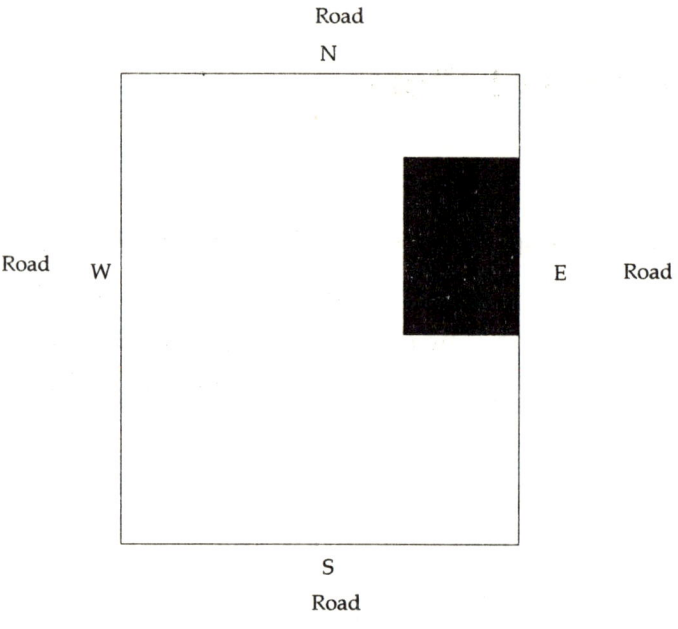

East-facing plot

2. A north-facing plot is also good.

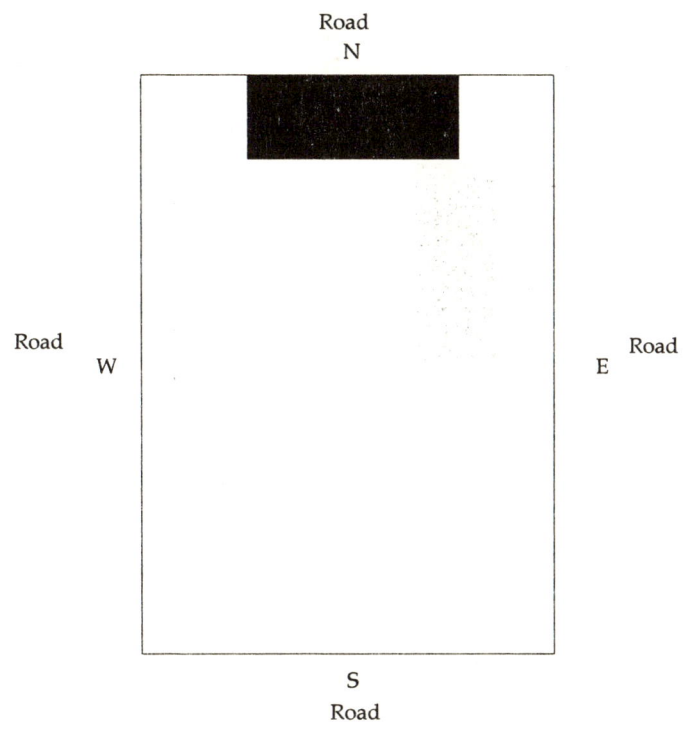

North-facing plot

3. Businessmen will benefit from a west-facing plot.

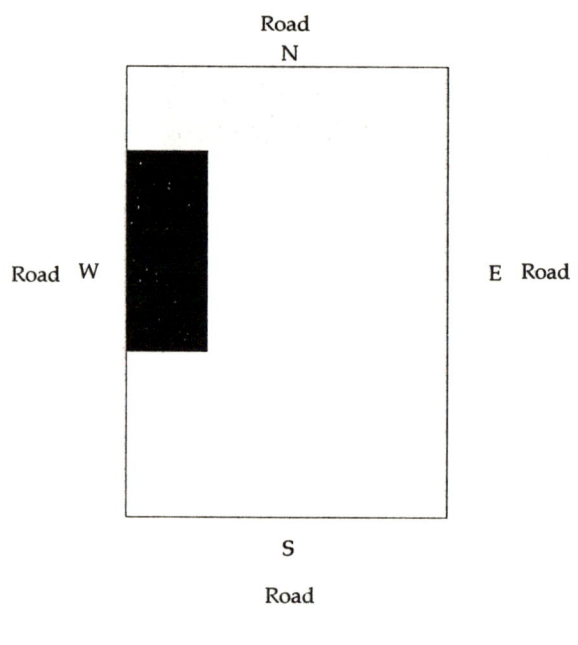

West-facing plot

4. People in entertainment business will be successful with a south-facing plot.

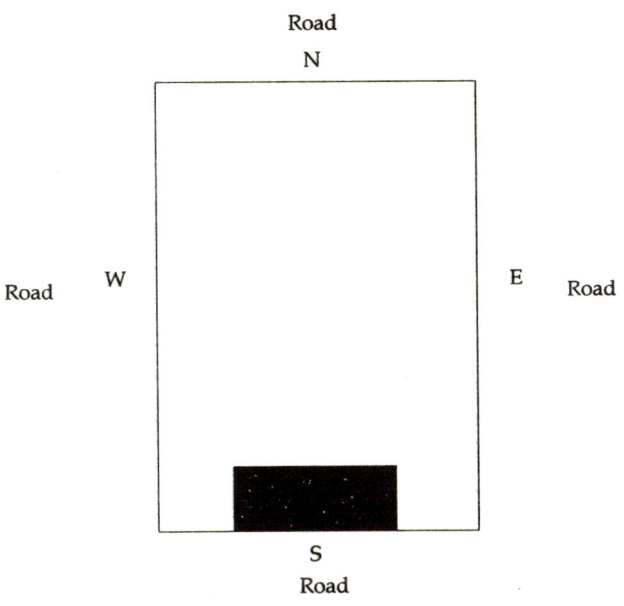

South-facing plot

5. The north-south area should be longer than the east-west area.

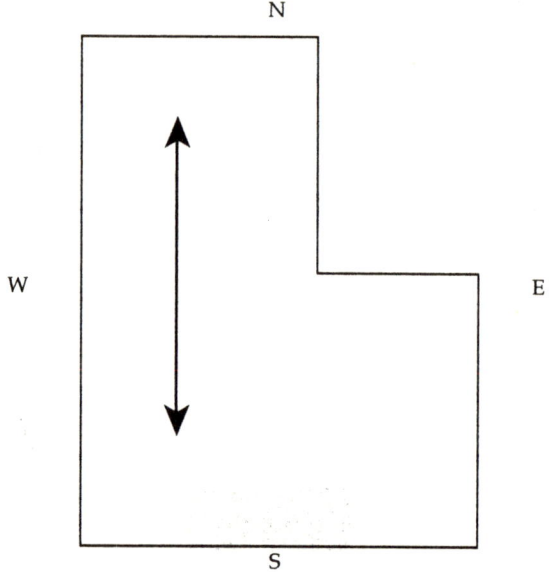

North-south longer than the east-west area

6. The ground should be sloping towards the north and east directions.
7. Since we get solar energy from the east, and the earth's magnetic axis runs north-south, the north-east position is considered special and a very good direction for construction purposes.

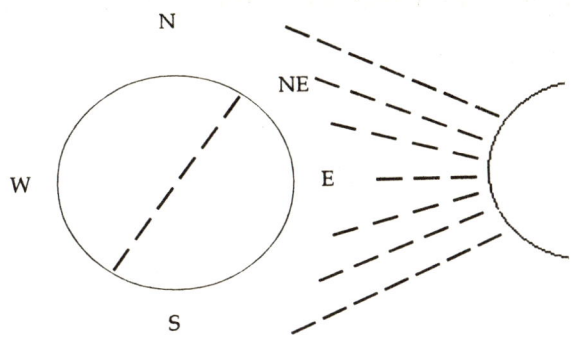

North-east – very good for construction

8. A plot with roads on all four sides is considered excellent.

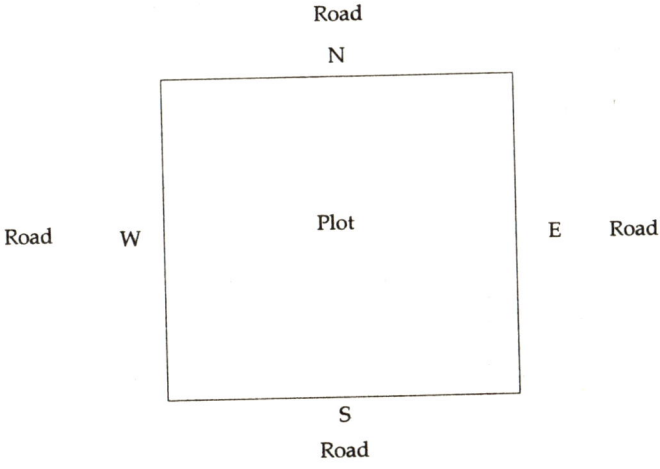

Plot with roads on all sides

9. A plot with roads along the north and east is also considered to be good.

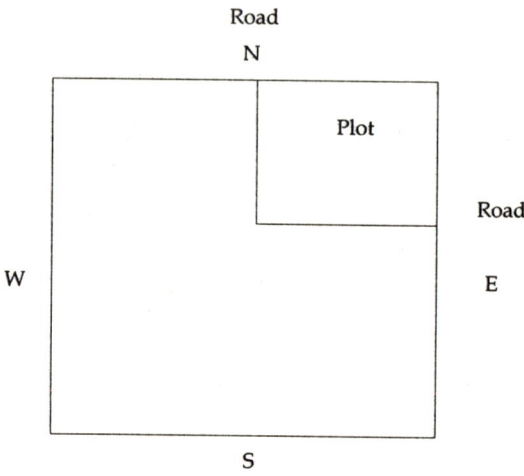

Plot with roads in the north and east

10. If there are bifurcated roads on all sides the plot is not good.

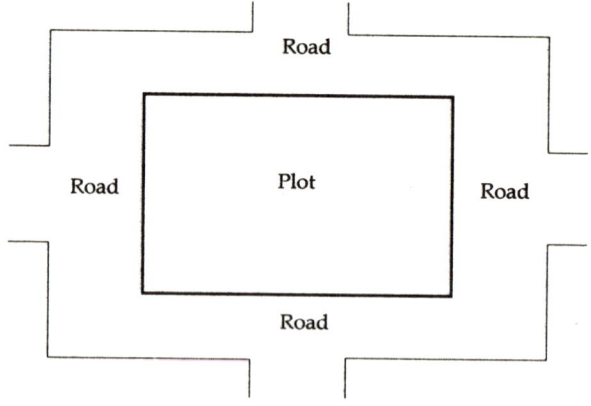

Plot with bifurcated roads

11. If there is a hill, a mountain, a tall building, or tall trees in the west or south-west, the plot is considered auspicious.

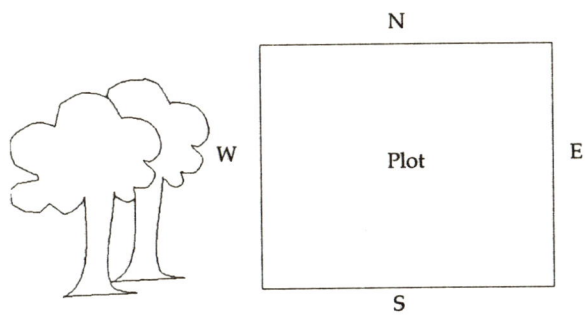

Tall trees in the west

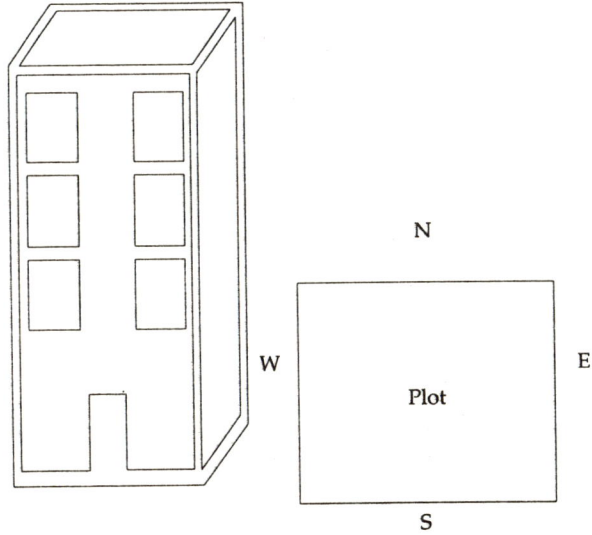

Tall building in the west

12. A plot should be either square or rectangular in shape.

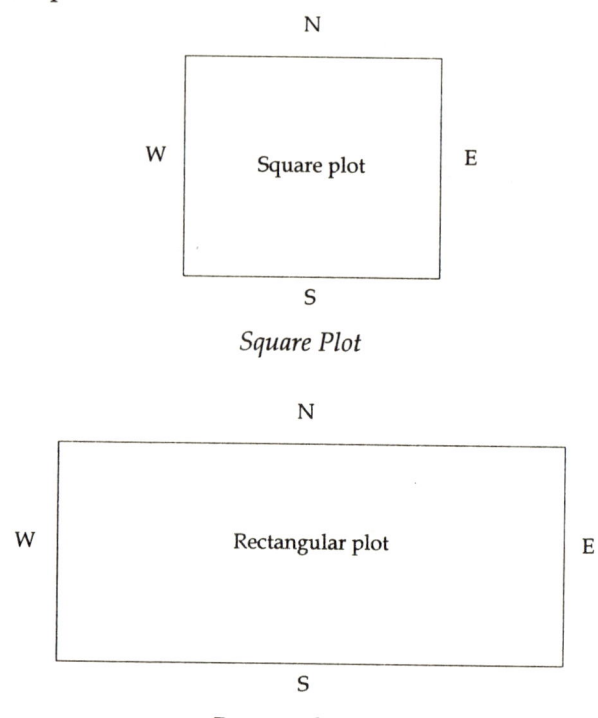

Square Plot

Rectangular plot

13. Yellow soil with a tinge of red is ideal.
14. The soil should have a pleasant, earthy smell.
15. If you dig a pit 3 ft deep, 3 ft wide and 3 ft long, fill it up with the earth that was dug out, and the filled earth forms a mound, or is in level with the surrounding ground, the plot is considered good.
16. A plot with its axis parallel to the earth's magnetic axis is good.
17. A plot consisting of bones, rocks and anthills should be avoided.

18. A square plot with extensions in the north or east is good.

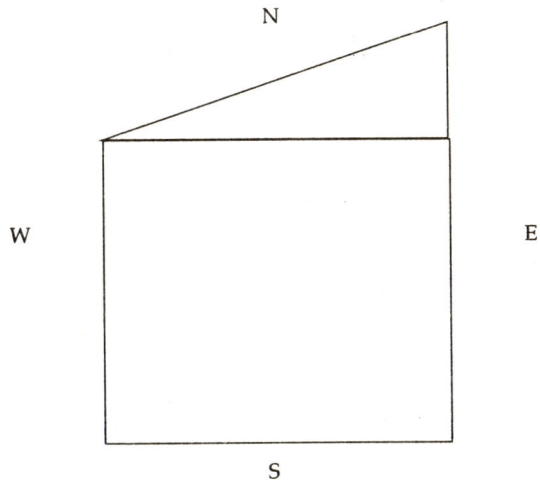

Square plot with extension in the north

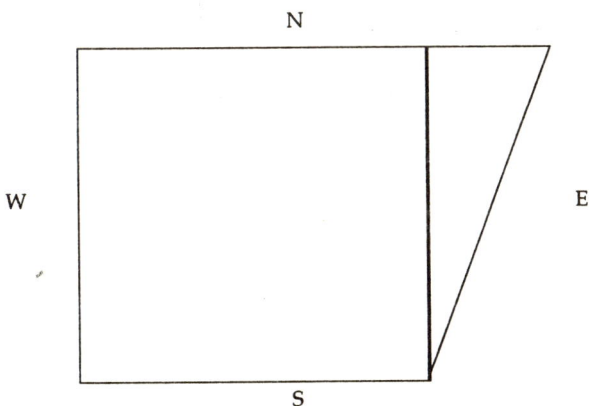

Square plot with extension in the east

19. A plot which has its north-west, or south-west, or even south-east cut off, can be rectified the Vaastushastra way, by bifurcating the plot as shown in the following diagrams:

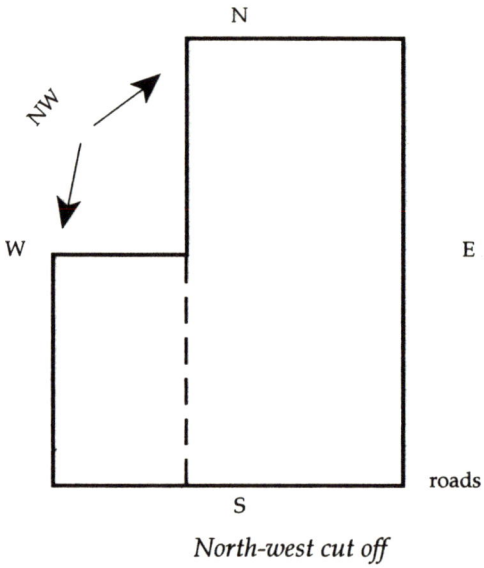

North-west cut off

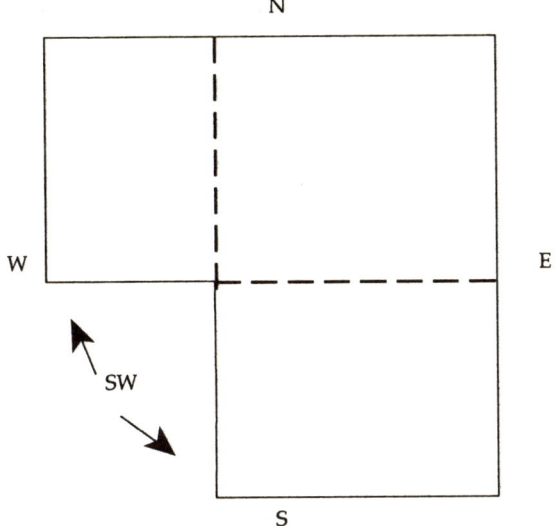

South-west cut off

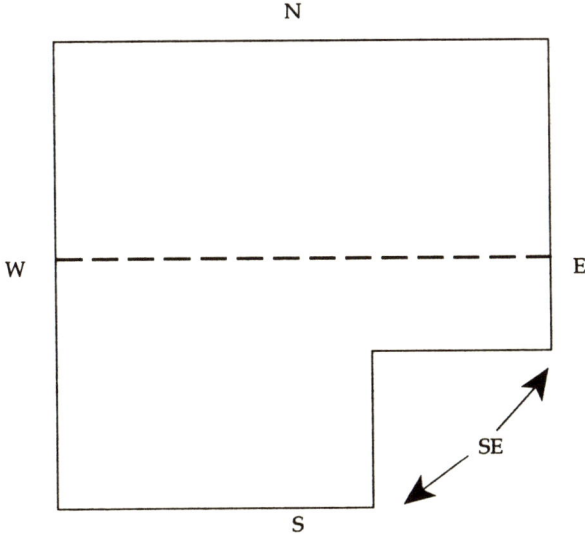

South-east cut off

20. In diagonal plots, where the plot faces either the north-east, north-west, south-east or south-west, the house should be built parallel to the adjacent roads.

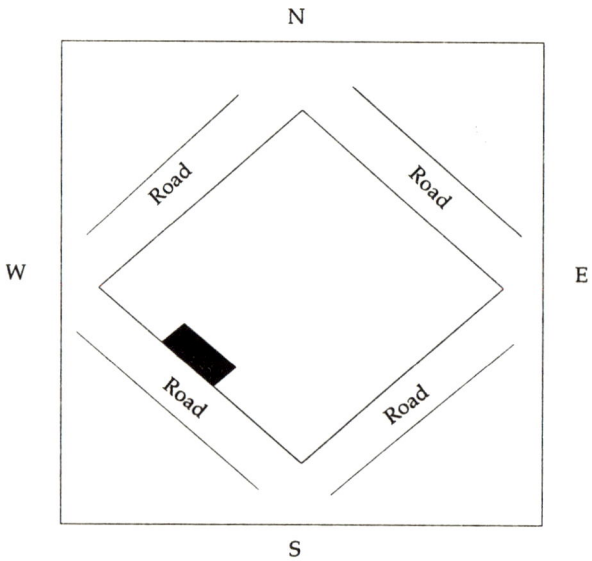

Plot facing south-west

21. In case you have a rectangular plot, see that its length is not more than twice its breadth.

```
┌─────────────────┐
│                 │
│                 │
│                 │
│ Rectangular Plot│
│                 │
│                 │
│                 │
└─────────────────┘
```

Length not more than twice breadth

22. Avoid a small plot which lies between two big plots.

Small plot between two big plots

23. If you buy a corner plot, ensure that it is a north-east corner one.

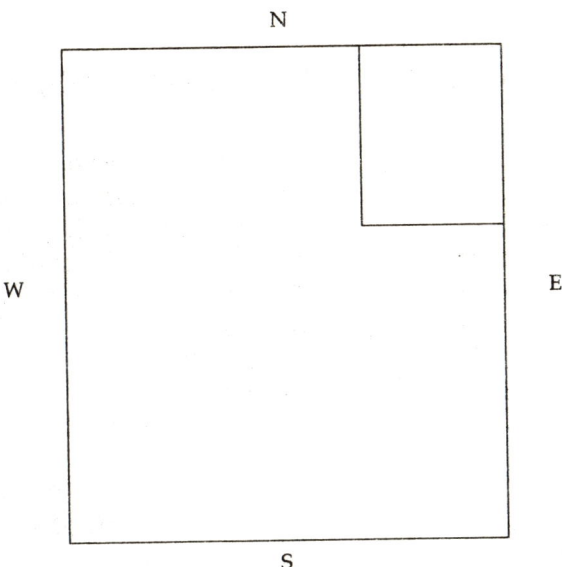

Plot in the north-east corner

Houses and Flats

1. When digging of the plot for laying the foundation commences, it should start with the north-east corner, then the north-west, the south-east, and finally the south-west.

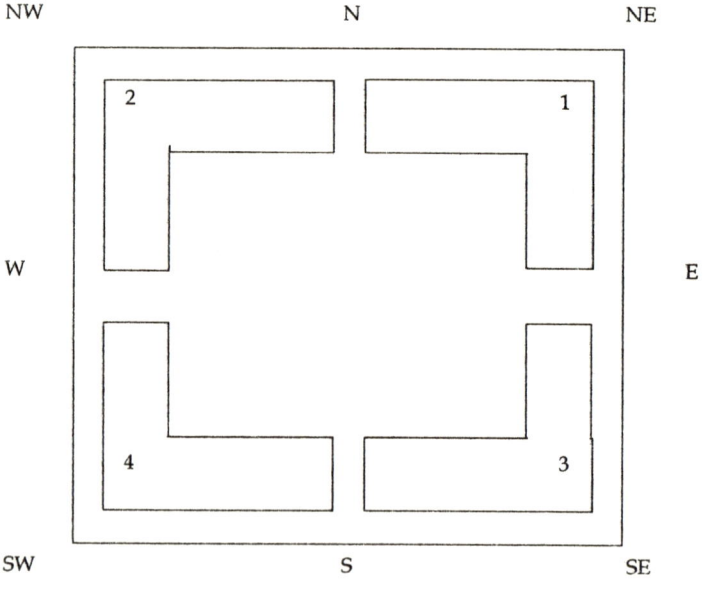

Digging for foundation

2. Laying the foundation should commence from the south-west corner, then proceed to the south-east, and north-west, and end with the north-east corner.

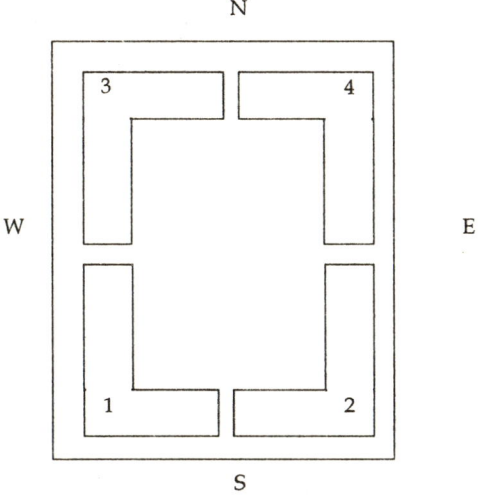
Foundation laying

3. While constructing a house, maximum area of the plot in the north-east should be kept open to receive plenty of sunshine.

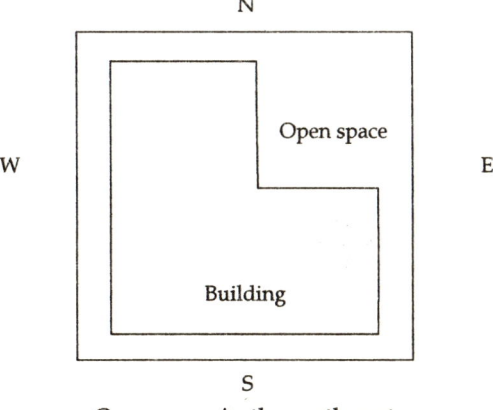
Open space in the north-east

4. The water-source should be in the north-east quarter of the plot.

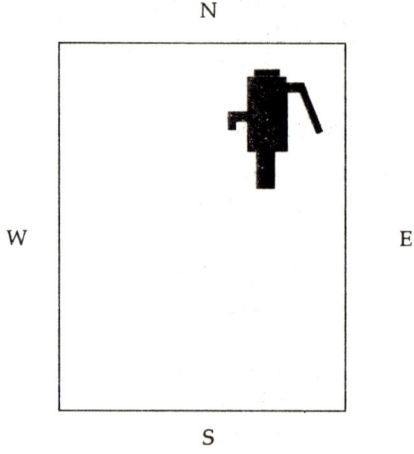

Water source in the north-east

5. If you have an overhead tank, then build it in the south-west quarter of the plot.

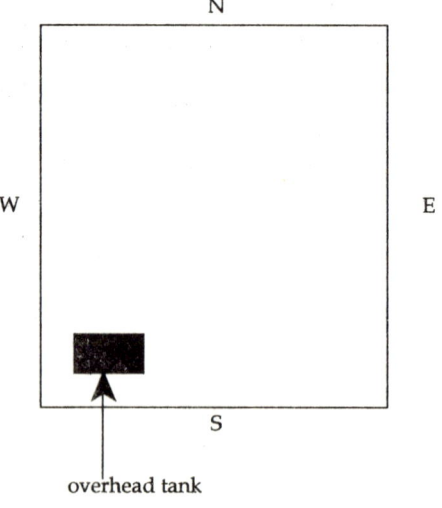

Overhead tank in the south-west

6. The building should either be square or rectangular in shape for a house or flat.

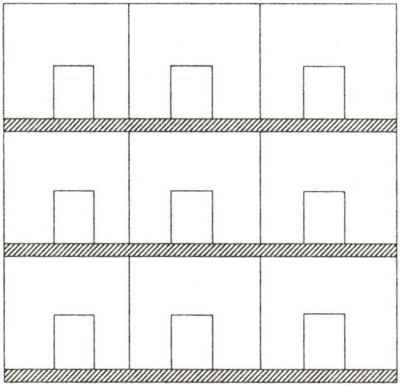

Square building for flats

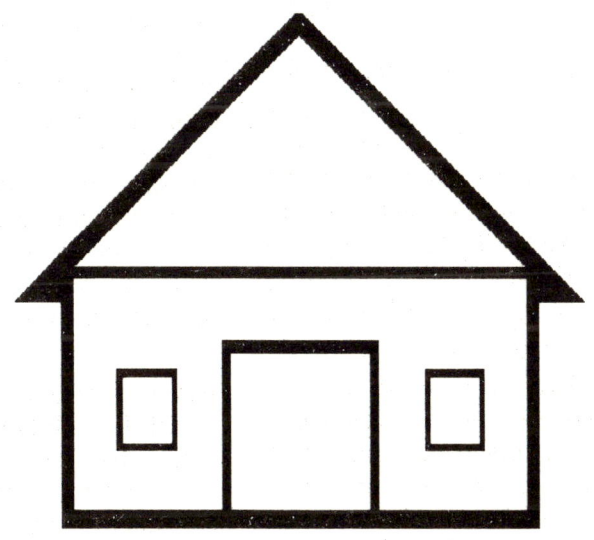

Rectangular house

7. The greater the height of the building, the better.
8. Since steel or reinforced cement – concrete, provided in the slab, affect the electromagnetic environment in the room, it is always better to have a high roof.
9. Avoid any beam crossing the room.
10. Do not build a column in the centre of the room.
11. Maximum use of wood and other non-magnetic metals like brass or aluminium is recommended.
12. The ground level of the plot should be equal or higher than the adjoining areas.
13. The plinth level should be at least 1½ to 2 ft higher than the area with highest ground level in the plot.
14. The foundation of the building should be equal to or lower than the adjoining foundations, at least 4 to 6 ft below the existing ground level.
15. It is ideal to have more doors, windows and balconies in the north and east direction of the house or building.

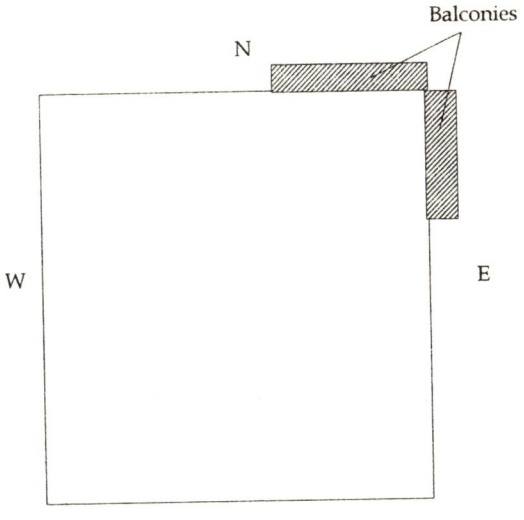

Balconies in the east and north

16. Place a lot of plants in the balconies if they are located in the south-west direction.

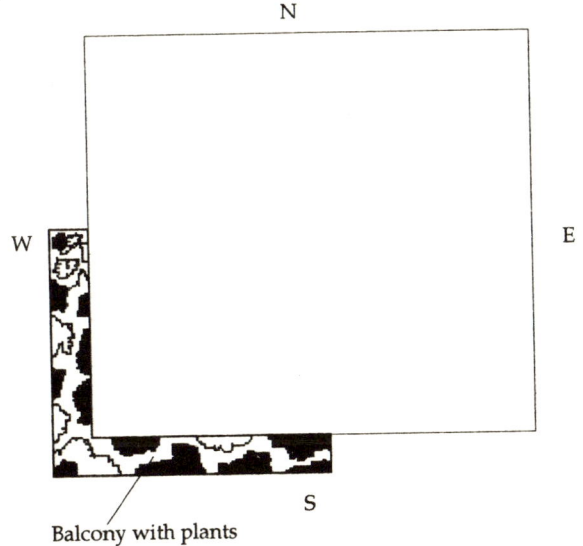

Balcony with plants in the south-west

17. The entrance door should be the biggest door in the house, having a length twice the breadth.

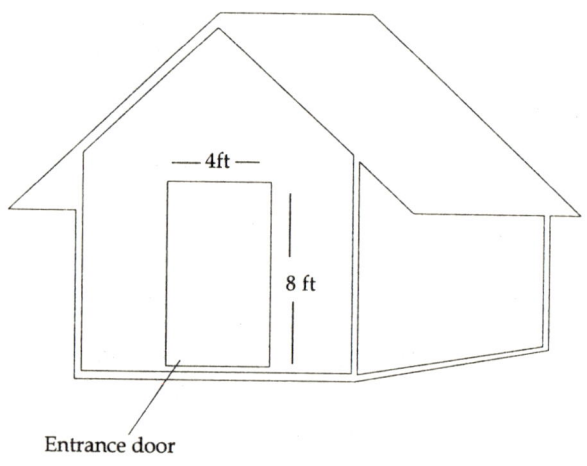

Entrance door with length twice the breadth

18. A flight of steps to the main door is beneficial.

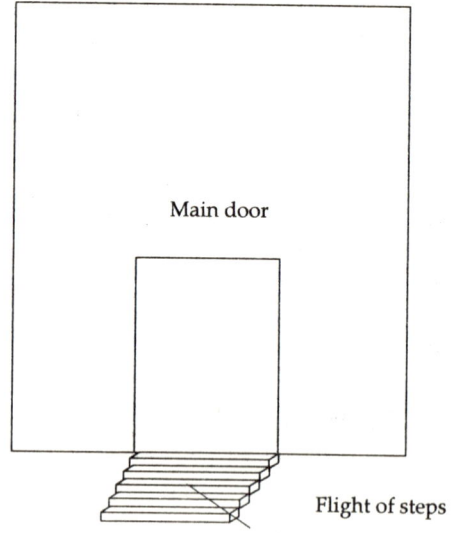

Flight of steps to main door

19. Avoid having the entrance and exit doors directly opposite each other as whatever positive energy comes in, will go out.

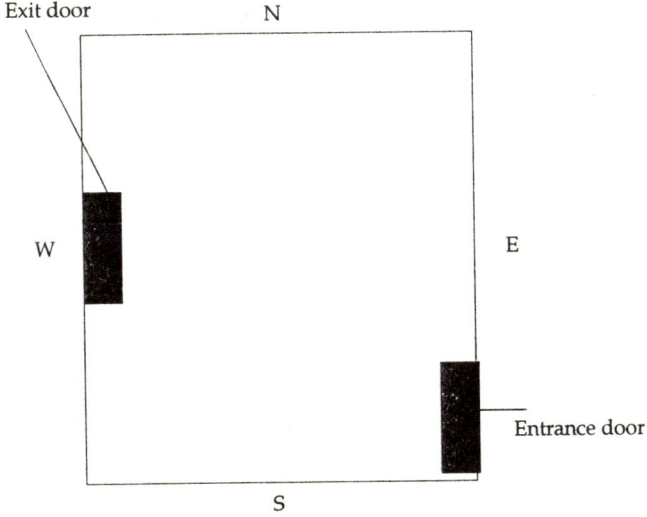

Entrance and exit doors

20. The rooms in the northern side should be bigger than those in the south, by at least 6 to 9 inches, but shorter in height by 1 to 3 inches.

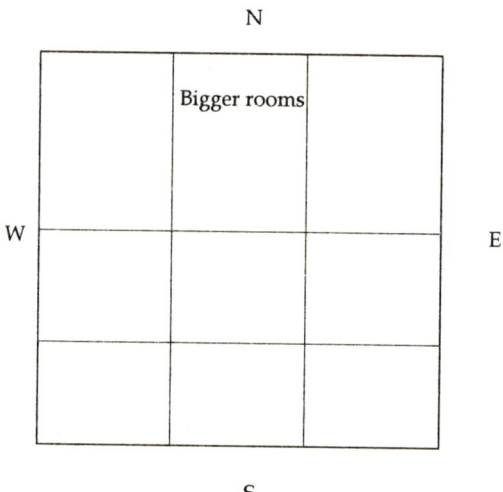

Bigger rooms in the north

21. The doors should be at least 7 ft in height, with the width being 3 ft 6 inches.

22. The window sill should be at least 3 ft 6 inches from the floor level.

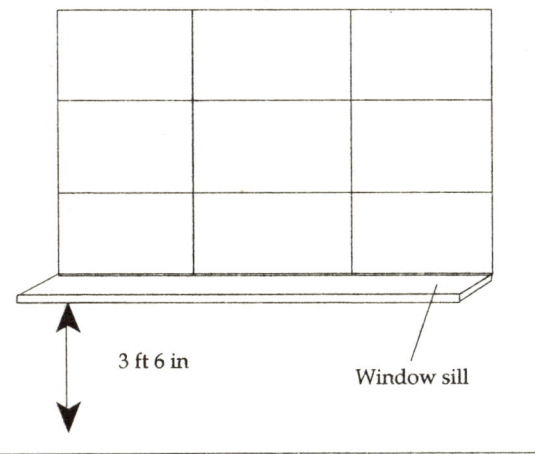

Window sill 3ft 6in from ground

23. Windows opening towards the north or east are the best.

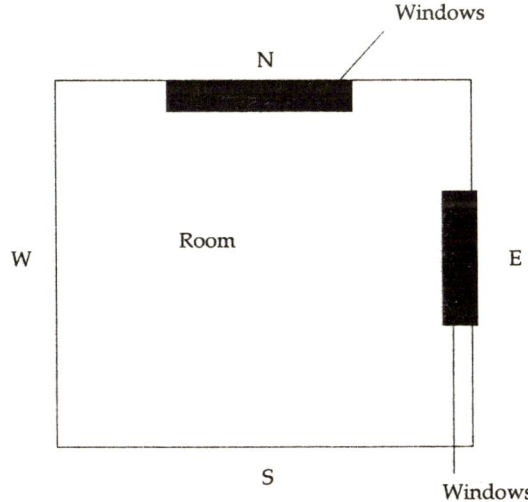

Windows in the north and east

24. Different levels for different rooms in a house should be avoided.
25. If you use sloping roofs, the slope should be towards the north, north-east or east.

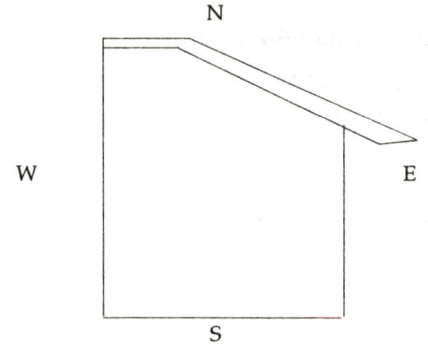

Roof sloping to the east

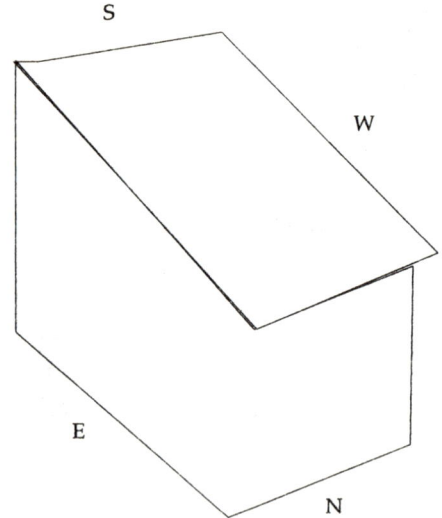

Roof sloping to the north

26. If possible, an extra room or storey should be constructed in the south or the west.

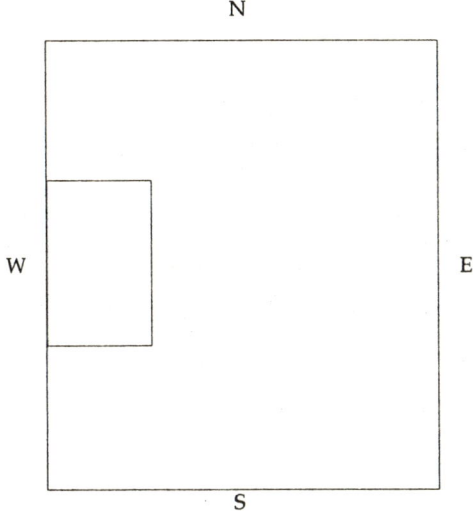

Extra room in the west

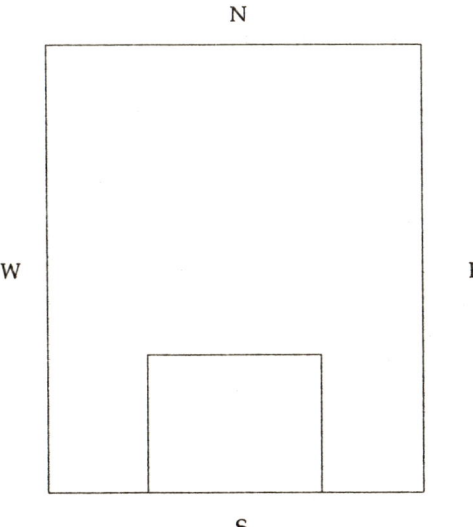

Extra room in the south

27. The walls on the north, north-east and east should be decorated with pictures, paintings, curios, wallpapers, etc.
28. The master bedroom should be in the south-west quarter, preferably in the corner, with the floor level 6 inches above the rest of the house.

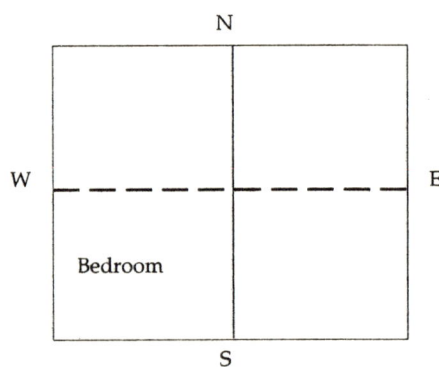

Master bedroom in the south-west quarter

29. Sleep with your head towards the south, or you can sleep in the east-west direction.

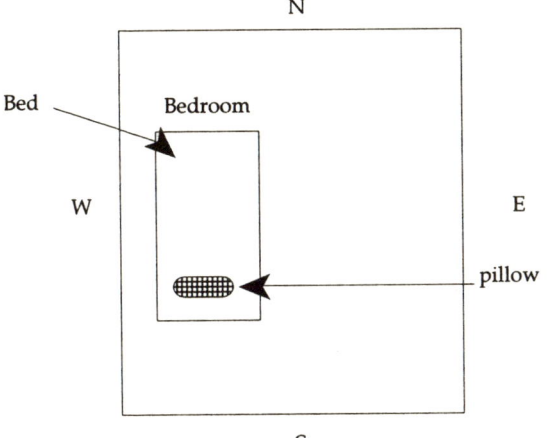

Sleeping with head towards the south

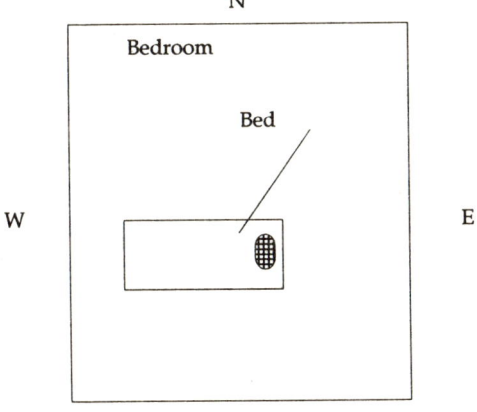

Sleeping in the east-west direction

30. The rooms in the north, north-east and east should be painted with bright, glossy colours, while dull, matt-finish colours would be advisable for the south and west rooms.

31. It is suitable to have the children's room in the north-west or south-east part of the house.

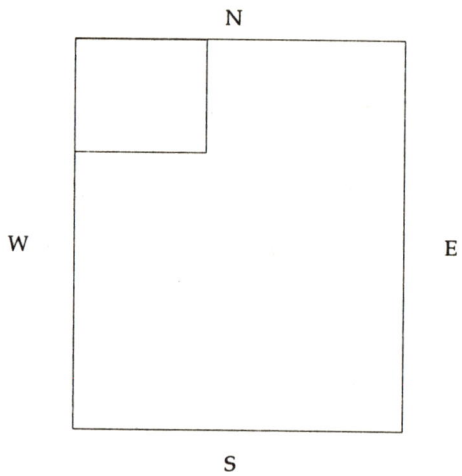

Children's room in the north-west part of house

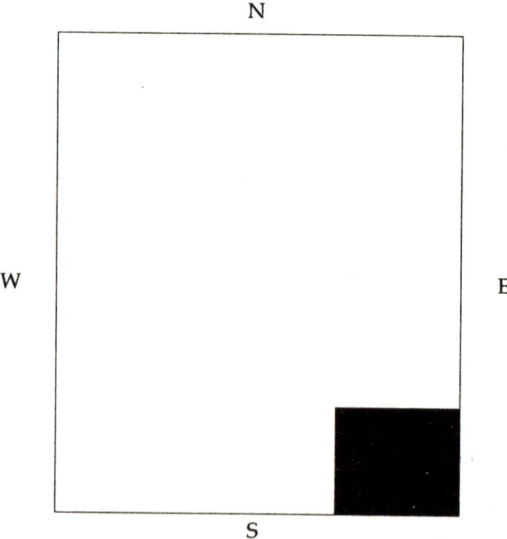

Children's room in the south-east part of house

32. The guest room should ideally be located in the north-west corner of the house, but can also be along the north-east side.

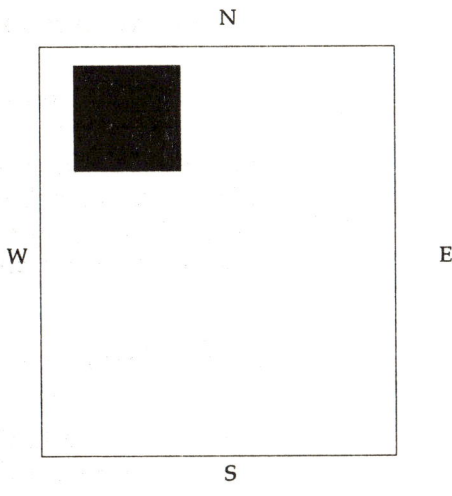

Guest room in the north-west

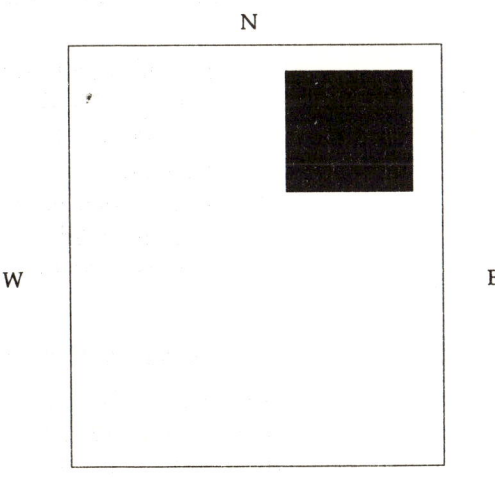

Guest room in the north-east

33. The best position for a prayer room is the north-east corner, followed by the east and north side.

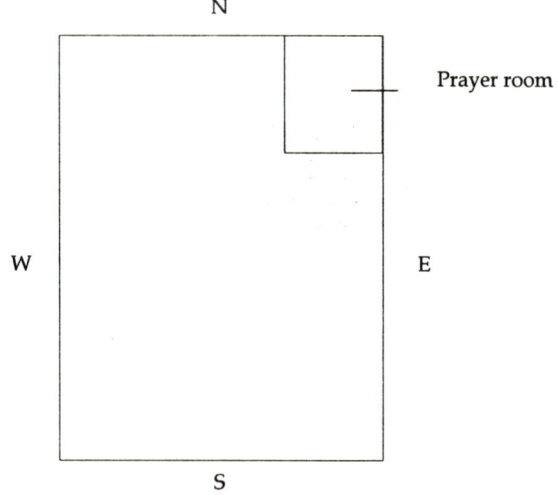

Prayer room in the north-east

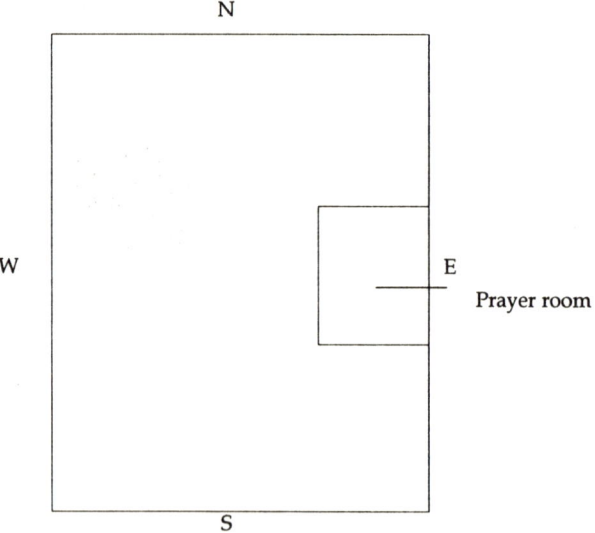

Prayer room in the east

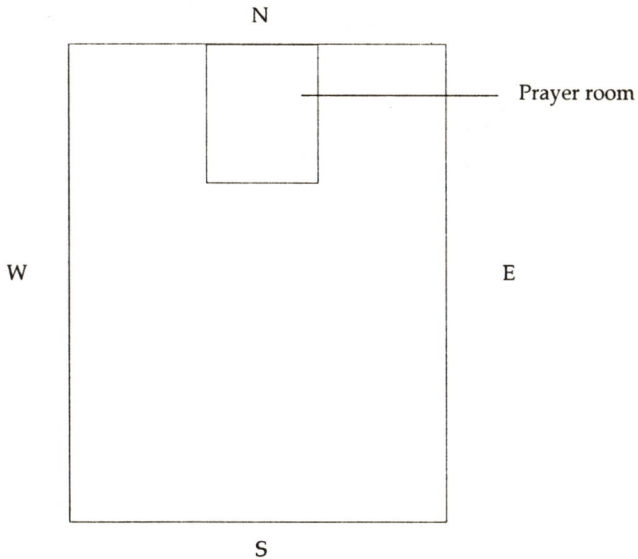

Prayer room in the north

34. A square prayer room, with its roof sloping from the centre on all sides is considered best for meditation and mental relaxation.

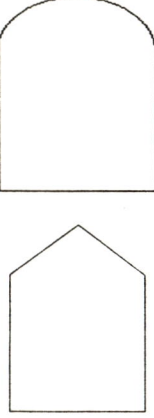

Roof sloping from the centre

35. Ideally, curtains should not be used to partition the prayer room.
36. It is ideal to have the drawing or living room in the north side.

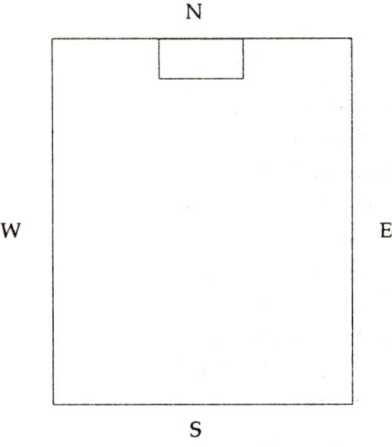

Drawing room in the north

37. The dining room is best located in the east of the house.

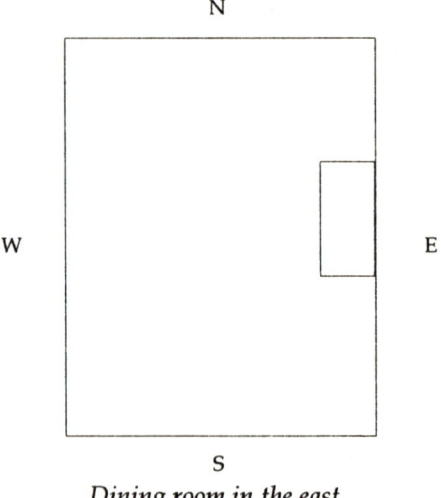

Dining room in the east

38. The furniture in the drawing and dining rooms should be only square or rectangular in shape.

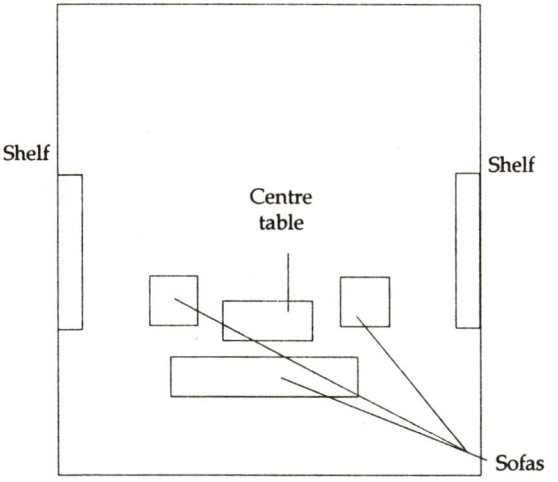

Square or rectangular furniture

39. Bathrooms and toilets should be located in the north-west or west.

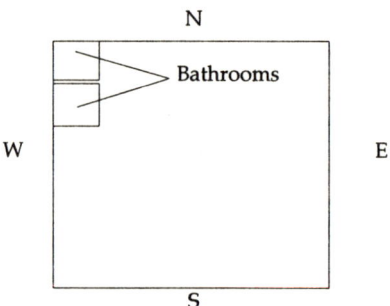

Bathrooms in the north-west

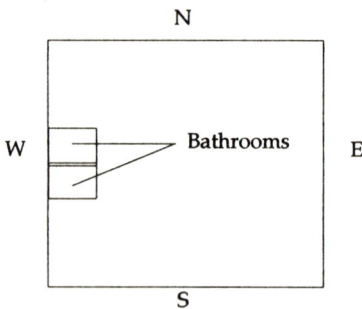

Bathrooms in the west

40. A storeroom is best situated in the south side.

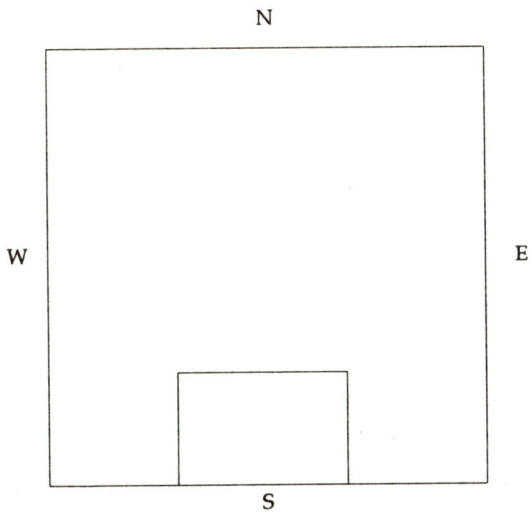

Storeroom in the south

41. The central portion of the building, if space permits, should be left open to the sky.
42. The staircase to the upper floor is ideal in the south-west corner.

43. The kitchen should be located in the south-east corner.

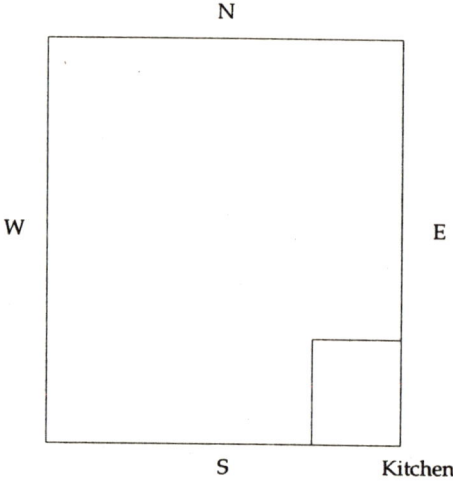

Kitchen in the south-east corner

44. The ideal side for a basement is the north-east quarter, but you can also have it in the north-west or the south-east.

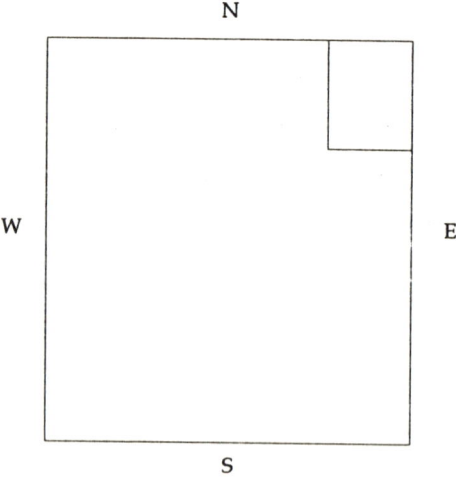

Basement in the north-east

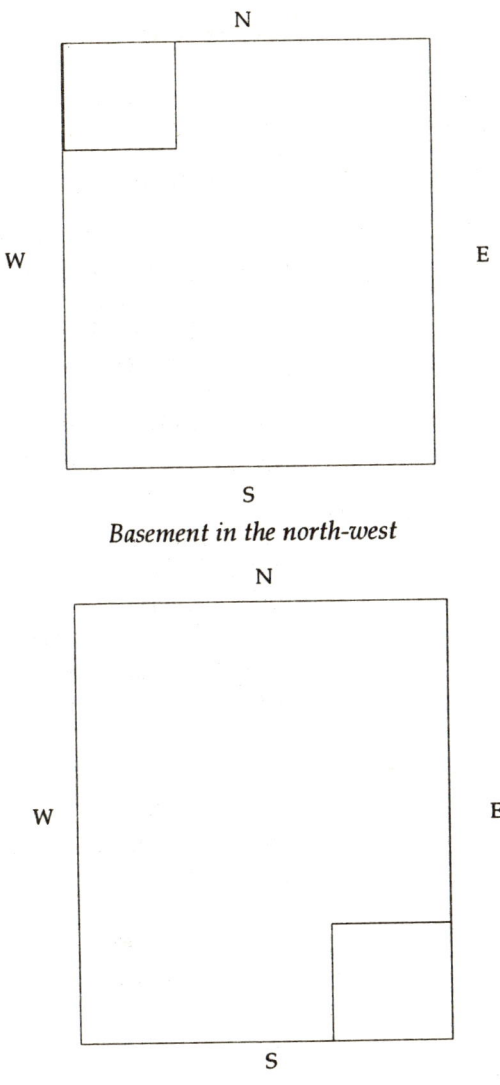

Basement in the north-west

Basement in the south-east

45. A mezzanine in the north-east is best avoided.
46. Do not construct the kitchen, toilets and prayer room next to each other.

47. The kitchen should not be located in front of the main door.
48. The safe should face the north or east.
49. Avoid having a toilet or a fireplace in the north-east corner of the house.
50. Avoid having a toilet or a prayer room under a staircase.
51. The walls in the south-west of the house should be thicker than those in the north-east.
52. The aged will be more comfortable in the south-west corner of the house.

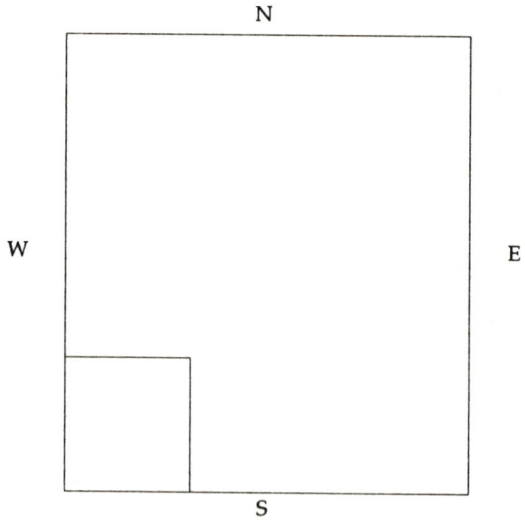

Room in the south-west for the aged

53. Avoid having cacti inside the house.
54. A basil plant in the front of the house is considered auspicious.

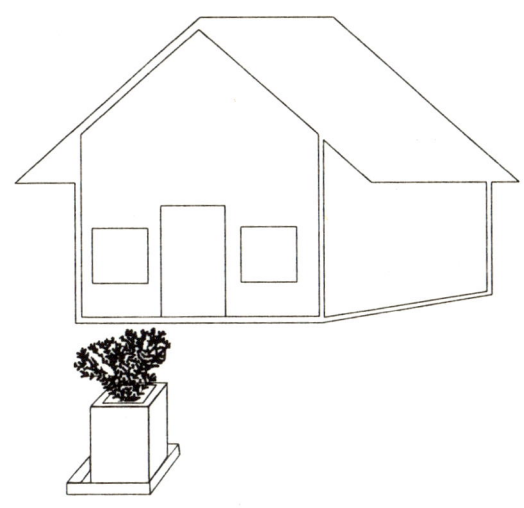

A basil plant in front of the house

55. It is the most ideal to locate the kitchen in the south-east quarter. The next best location is the north-west quarter.

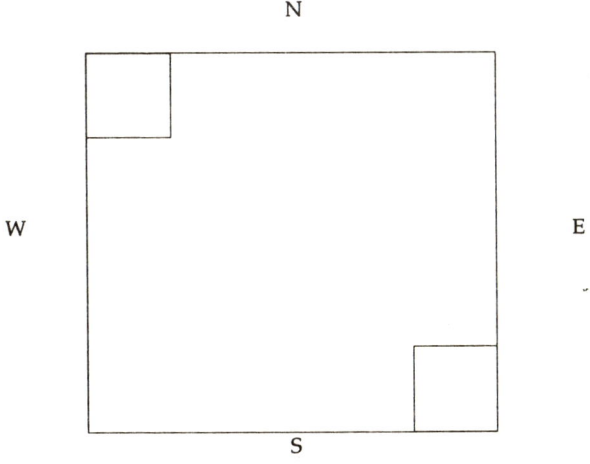

Kitchen in the north-west or south-east

56. More doors and windows should be on the ground floor.
57. Your main door should not be opposite the main door of another house.
58. The north-east walls are suitable for mirrors, wash-basins and taps.
59. The main gate should always be bigger than the doors in the building.
60. Cooking should be done, facing the east or the north.
61. The refrigerator should be placed in the north-west corner.
62. Rations can be stored along the south-west wall.

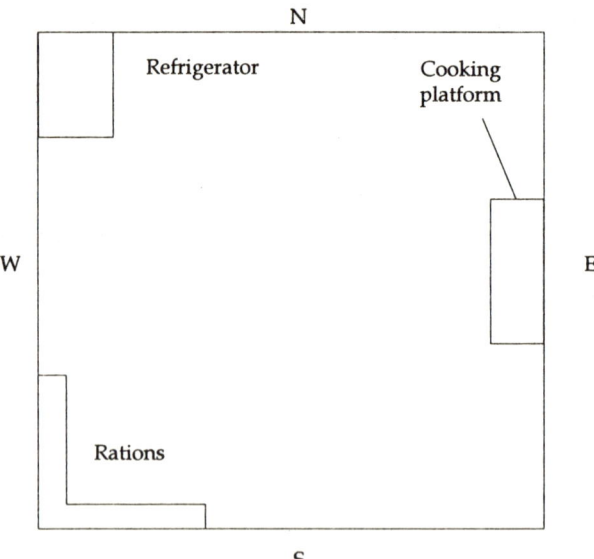

Kitchen arrangement

63. The main gate should preferably be towards the north-east of the plot for east and north-facing flats; north-west for west-facing plots; and south-west for south-facing plots.

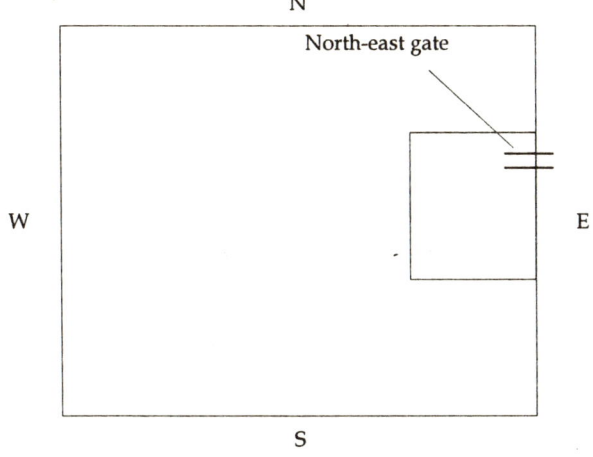

Main gate for east-facing plot

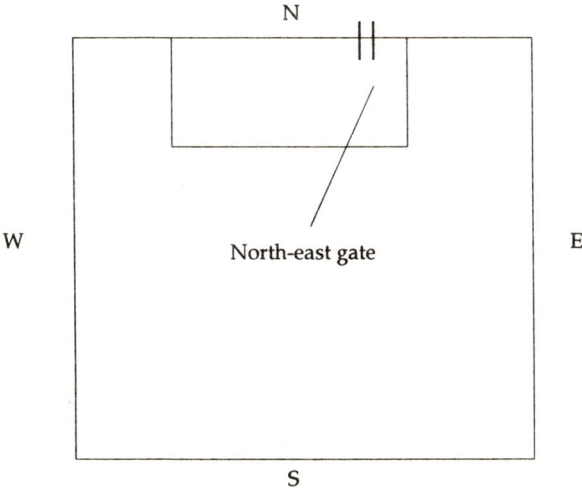

Main gate for north-facing plot

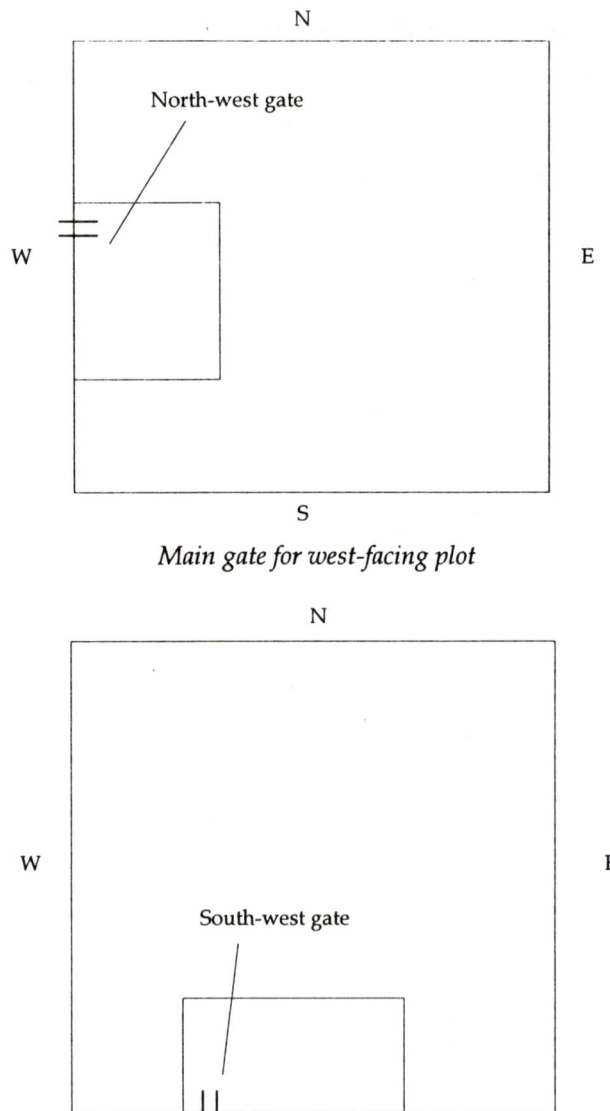

Main gate for west-facing plot

Main gate for south-facing plot

64. The main gate should always open inwards.

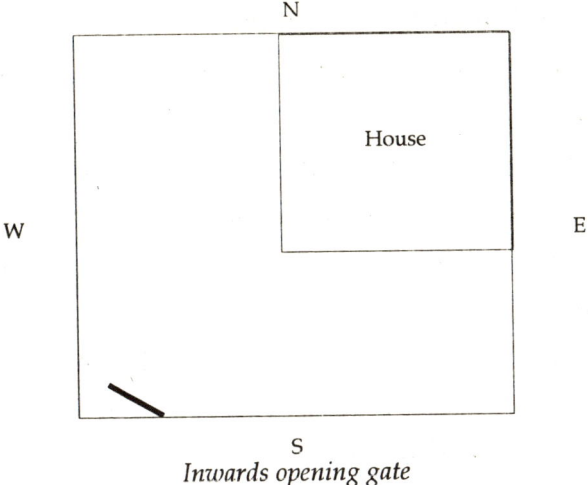
Inwards opening gate

65. Balconies are best in the north and east.

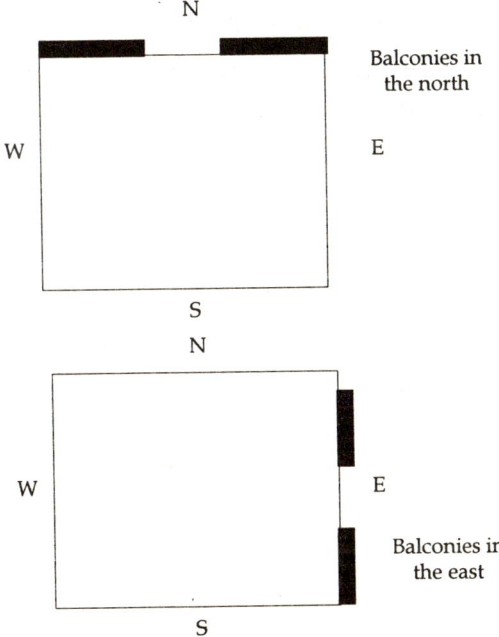
Balconies in the north and east

66. Avoid having a tree, temple, electric pole, open drain, hospital, court or jail in front of the entrance gate.
67. The compound wall in the south and west should be higher than in the east and north.
68. Open grills and railings would be good for balconies.
69. Flowering and medicinal plants thrive well in the east, north-east, north or north-west.
70. Tall trees in the south-east or south-west, and medium-height trees in the west or south grow well.
71. A servant's quarters, totally independent of the main building, should be located in the south-east or south corner of the plot.

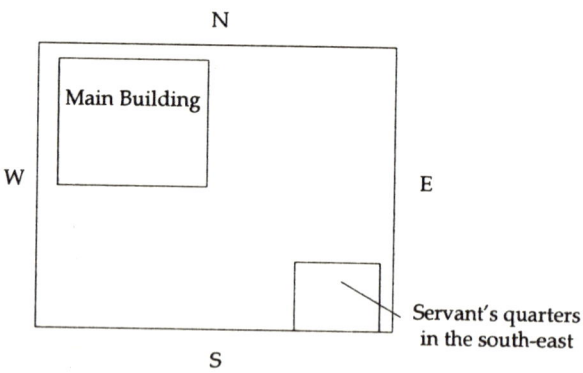

Servant's quarters in the south-east

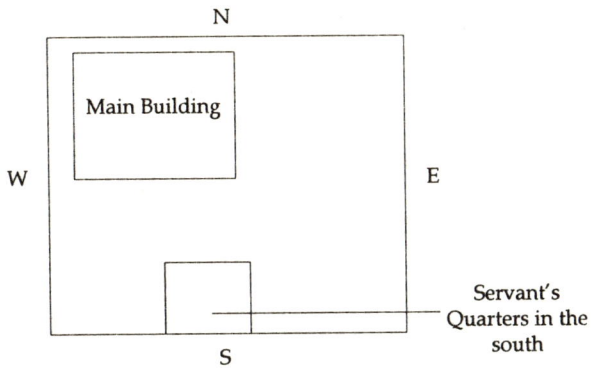

Servant's quarters in the south

72. A garage should best be built in the south-east or north-west corner.

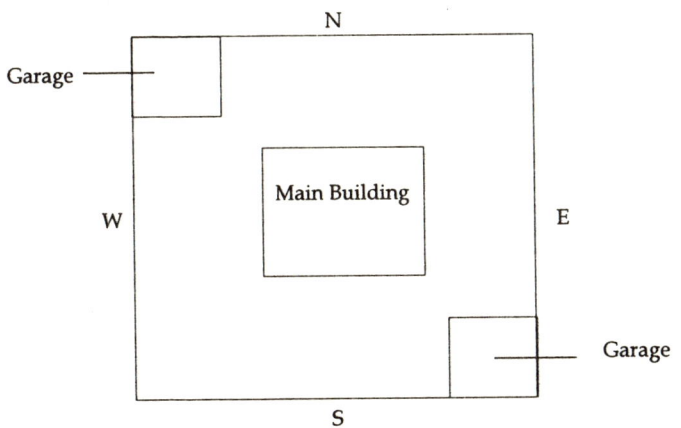

Garage in the north-west or south-east

73. If you wish to have a well dug, or a pump installed, the ideal place would be the north-east corner, or the north side of the plot.

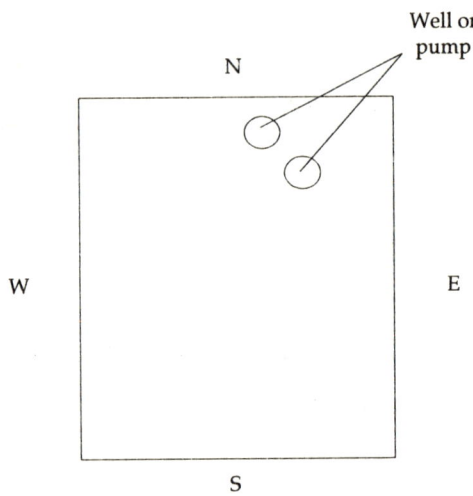

Well or pump in the north-east

The following diagram explains the benefits and ills of having wells or pumps in certain locations.

NW	N	NE
Injuries and loss	Happiness	Prosperity
Success	Extreme harm	Wealth and happiness
Misfortune	Misery for wife	Loss of son likely
SW	S	SE

Benefits or ills of wells or pumps in certain locations

74. Basements and cellars are ideal in the north, east or north-east direction.

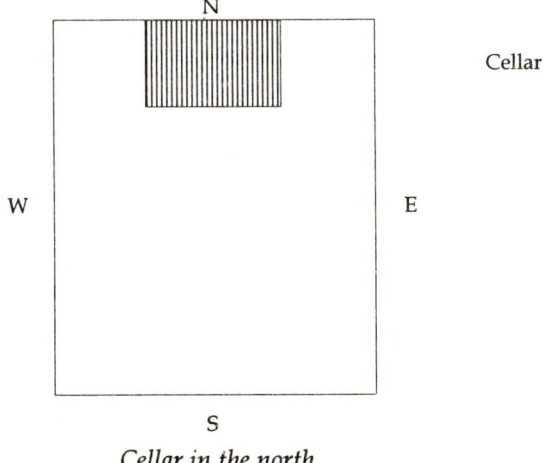

Cellar in the north

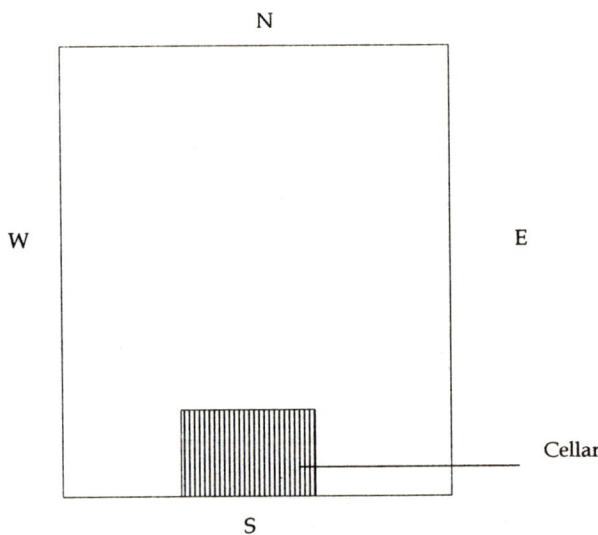

Cellar in the south

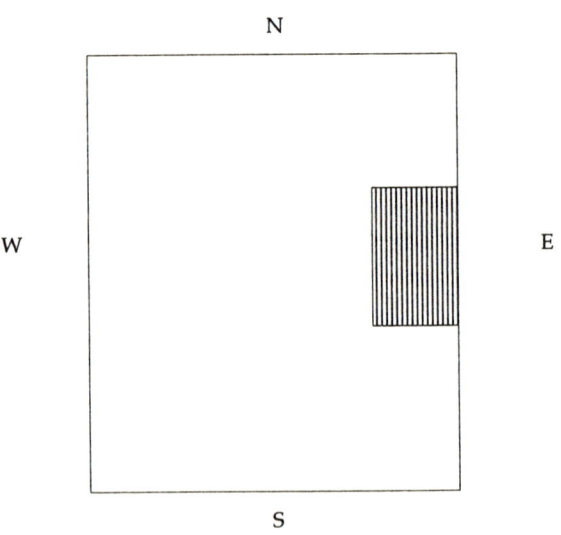

Cellar in the east

Shops and Offices

1. Shops with driveways and entrances in the east and north do well.

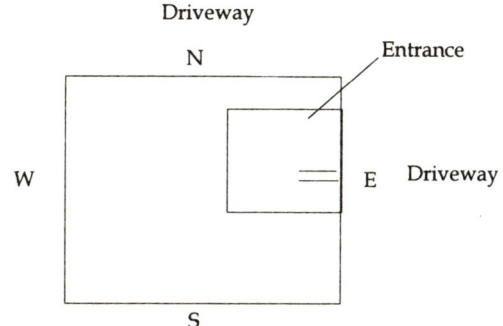

East-facing shop with entrance in the east

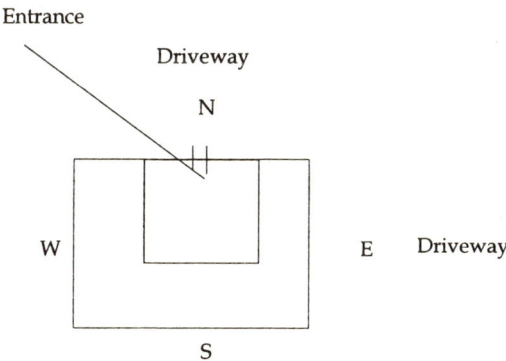

North-facing shop with north entrance

2. Those in the entertainment or food business should have their shops facing the west or south.

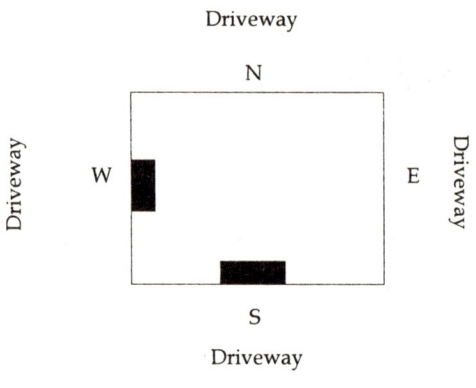

Shops facing west or south

3. The number of doors in an office or a shop should not be in multiples of ten.
4. The number of doors can be the same as your birth date reduced to a single digit, like 10th becomes 1, or any odd or even number according to your birth number.
5. For businessmen dealing in books, paper or educational goods, an east-facing shop is ideal.
6. For professionals, a north-facing office is suggested.

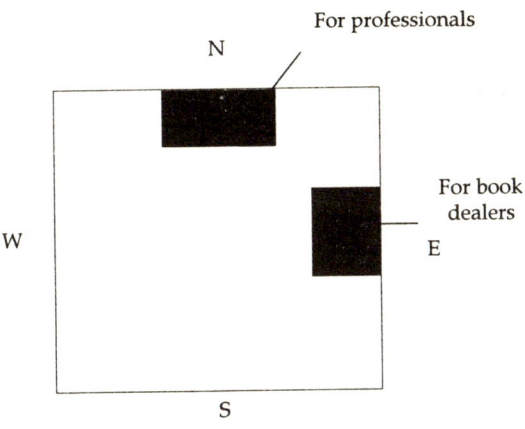

East-facing and north-facing offices

7. For businessmen dealing in fun-food and fashion items, the south-east or south corner shop or office is best.
8. The ideal location for shops dealing in black-coloured goods like coal, artificial leather goods, etc, would be the south.
9. Hotels, restaurants, electric goods shops would do good business in the south-east corner of the east side.
10. Business dealing with garments, and departmental stores will be successful in the east.
11. Agricultural business will flourish in the west.

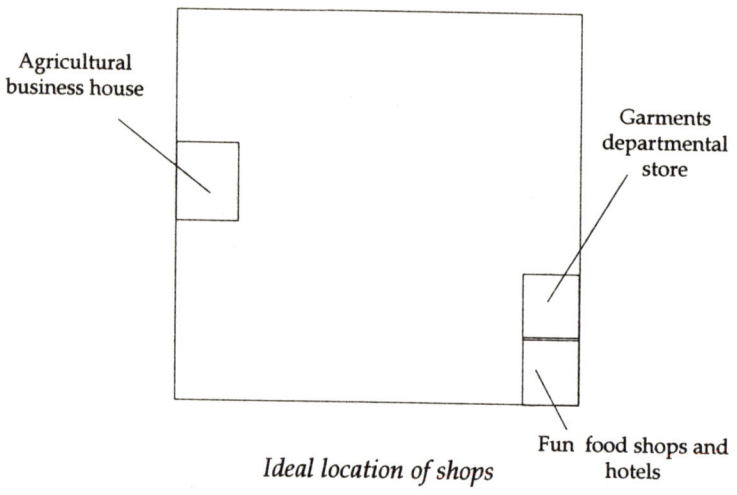

Ideal location of shops

12. Automobile business will excel in the east and north-west.

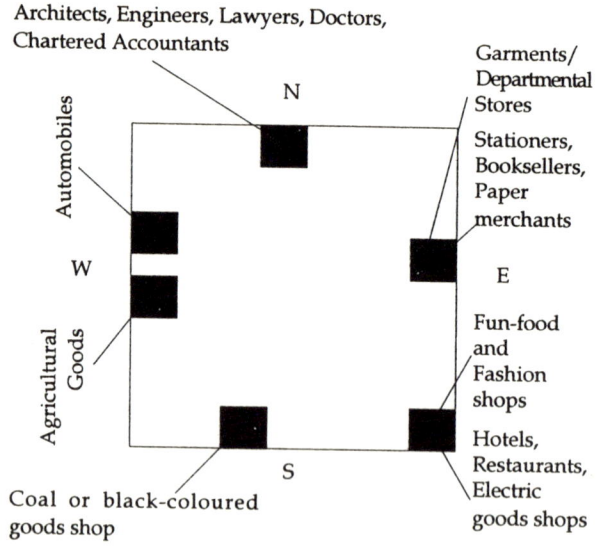

Ideal location for success in business

13. The showcases or racks should be in the south and west part of the shop.
14. The cash counter should be in the south-east side of the shop.

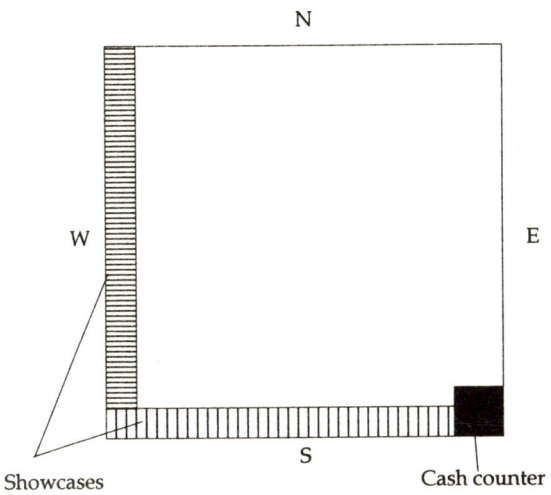

Showcases and counter in a shop

15. Ideally, wooden furniture should be used in shops.
16. There should be no cross-beams in a shop or office.
17. The electric meter or switchboard should be in the south-east corner.
18. The shop owner should sit facing the east or north.
19. Goods should be stocked along the south-west wall.
20. The cash box should be on the owner's right if he faces east, and on his left if he faces north.
21. The safebox should open to the north.

22. The accounts section in an office should be located in the north.

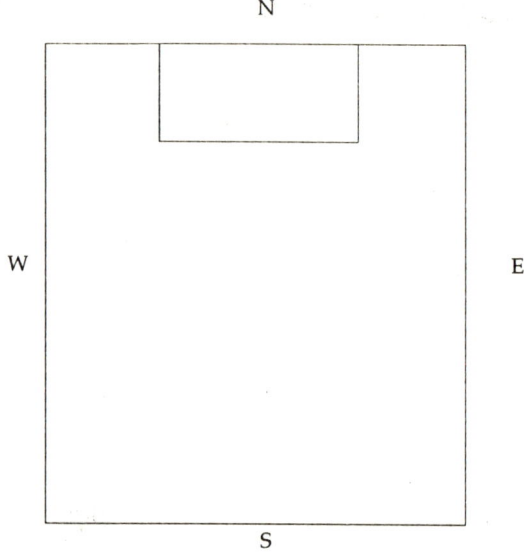

Accounts department in the north

23. The sales and marketing department should be located in the north-west corner of the office.

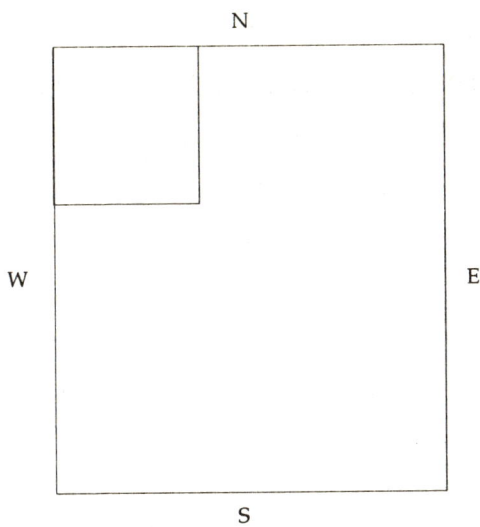

Sales and Marketing department in the north-west

24. The administration and personnel department should be located in the east.

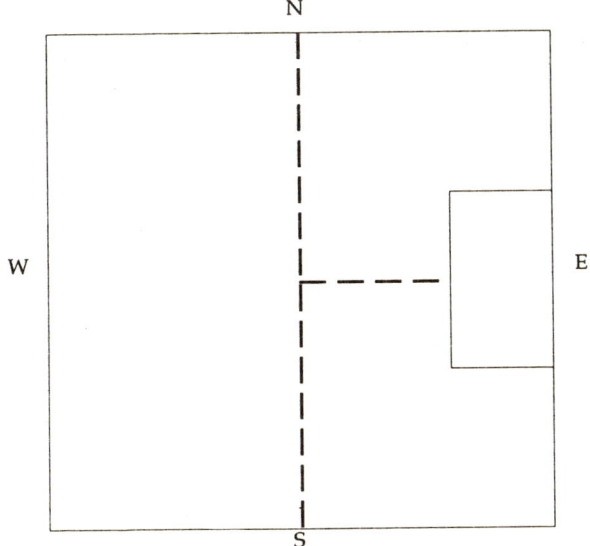

Administration and Personnel department in the east

25. The director's rooms should be in the south-west, with the floor 6 inches higher than the rest of the office floor.

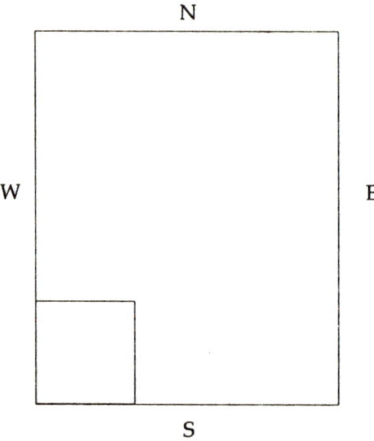

Director's room in the south-west

26. The water-cooler or filter in the office should be placed in the north-east side.

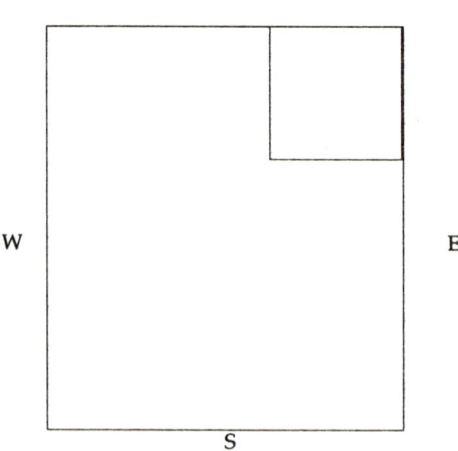

Water-filter in the north-east

27. The kitchen should be in the south-east corner.

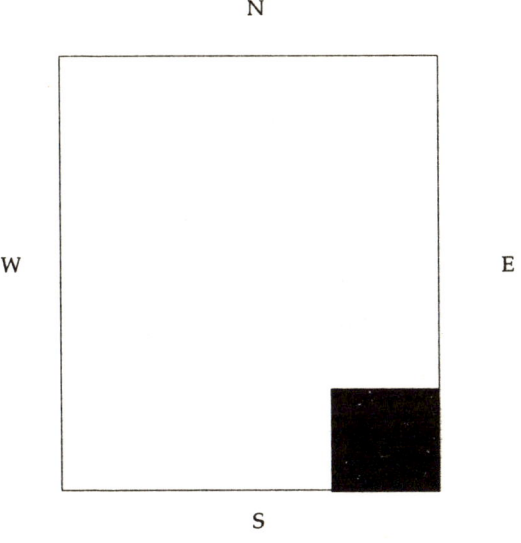

Kitchen in the south-east

28. Avoid having a toilet in the north-east side of a shop or office.
29. It is best to have the staircase along the south-west wall.

Other Buildings

Hotels and Restaurants

1. Hotels and restaurants are ideal in the south-east in a plot.

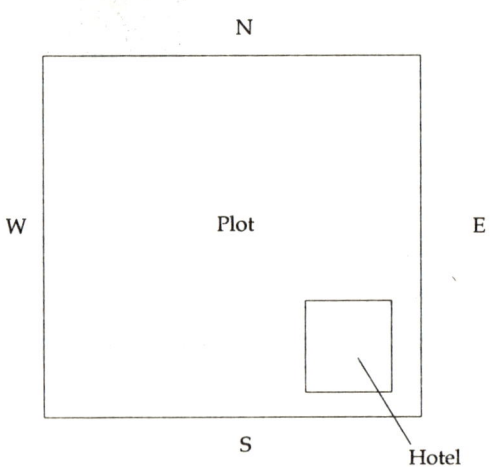

Hotel in the south-east

2. The kitchen in hotels should be in the south-east side of the building.

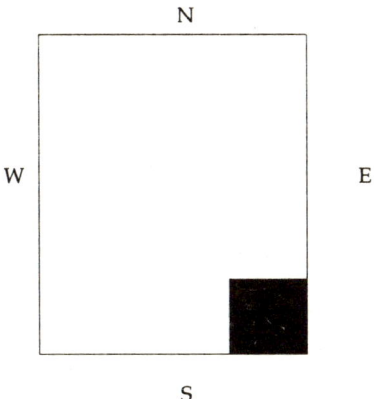

Kitchen in the south-east

3. Avoid using black tinted glasses.
4. Have enough ventilation for the dining area.

Religious Buildings

1. An east or north-facing plot is ideal for any religious building.

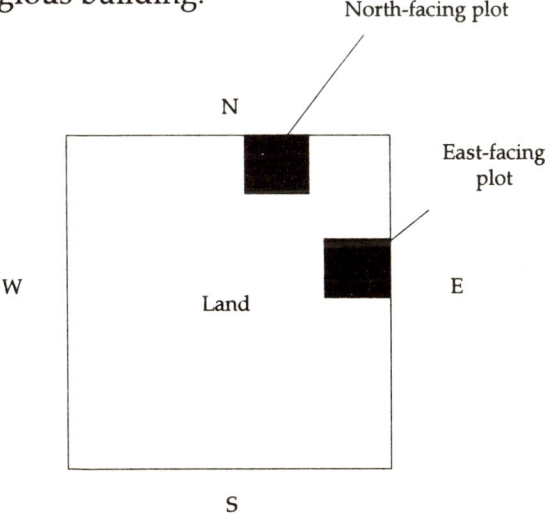

North-facing and east-facing religious buildings

2. A sea, river, dam, water tank, lake or any other feature to the east or north of the plot is considered good.
3. A building on a hill or any elevated place is ideal for a temple, church, mosque, etc.
4. Avoid having the shadow of any nearby building falling on a religious building.
5. It is advisable that there are no liquor or leather goods shops, hotels, cinema halls, lottery counters, etc, in front of a religious building.
6. Have a boundary built around the building.

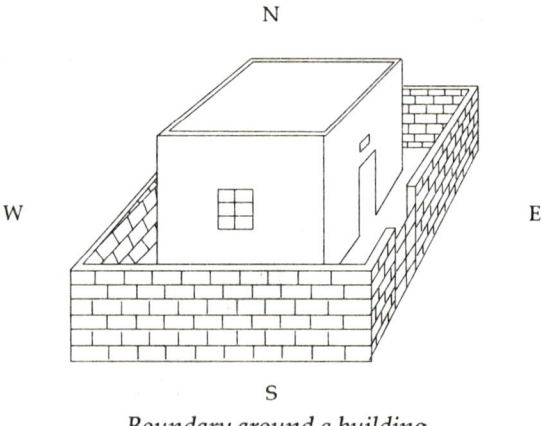

Boundary around a building

7. It is ideal to have the entrance gate on the east side of the compound.
8. The entrance gate should be taller than the other doors, and should be well-decorated.
9. Light and soothing shades of pastel colours like green, saffron, lemon yellow, or white should be used for pillars and flooring of the hall.
10. Toilets and bathrooms should be independent of the main building, and built in the east side.
11. A lotus pond or a fountain in the east or north-east is good.

Educational Institutions
1. The building should face the east or west.
2. The main entrance to the plot should either be in the east or in the north-east.
3. The main building should be in the south-west, south or west side of the plot.

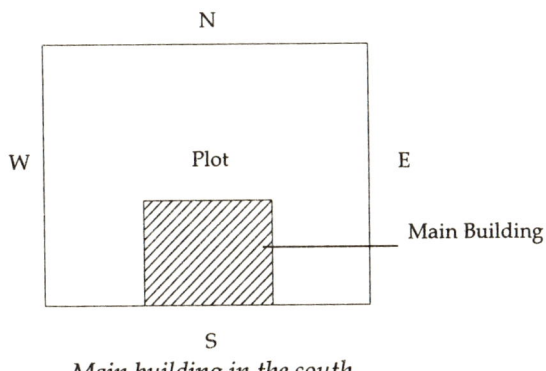

Main building in the south

4. The office room should be in the south-east side of the building, with doors in the north or east wall.

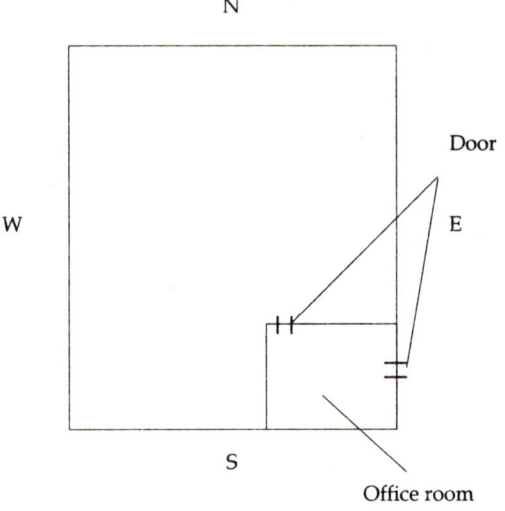

Office room in the south-east

5. The length of the classroom should be double the width of the room.

6. The blackboard should be placed in the west side of the room.

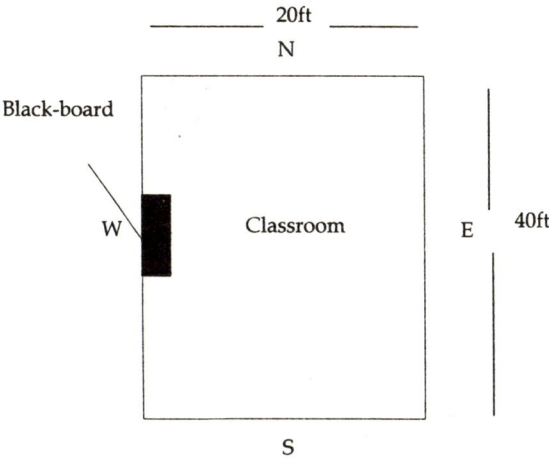

Classroom with blackboard in the west

7. The dais for the teacher's table and chair should be at least 1½ to 2 feet high.
8. Good ventilation and lighting are essential.

Hospitals and Clinics

1. An east-facing plot is ideal for hospitals and clinics.

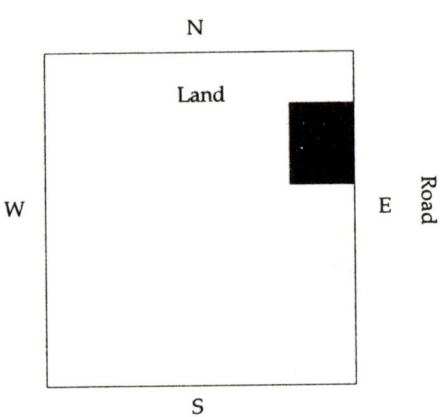

East-facing clinic

2. The building should be in the east side of the plot.

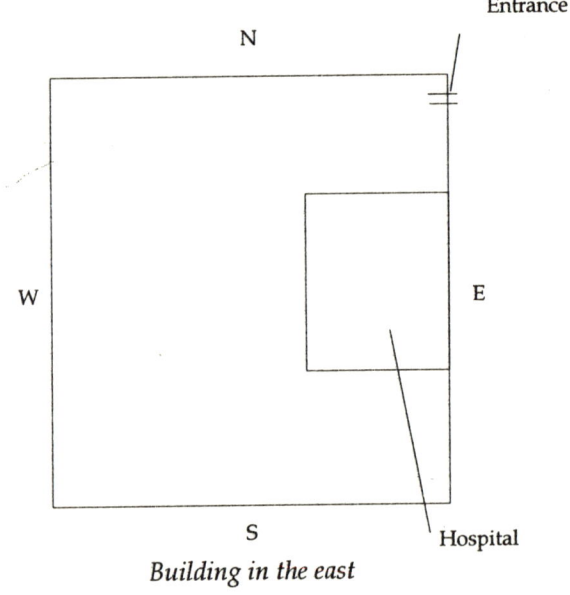

Building in the east

3. The main entrance to the plot should be in the east or the north-east corner.
4. The enquiry window should be facing the south-east.
5. The waiting room should be in the south side.
6. Patients should be checked in the room that is in the north side of the building.
7. Patients should be made to lie with their heads towards the south or west.

Factories

1. The plot should be east or north-facing.

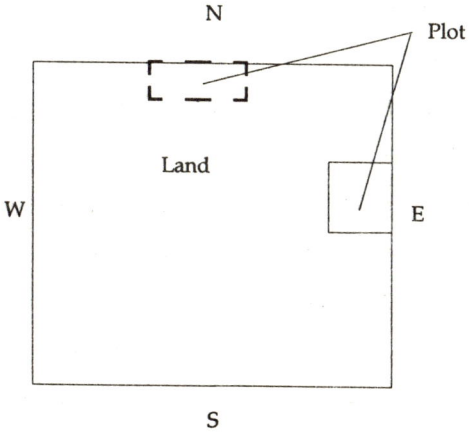

East or north-facing plot

2. The main office of the management should be in the south-west side of the plot.

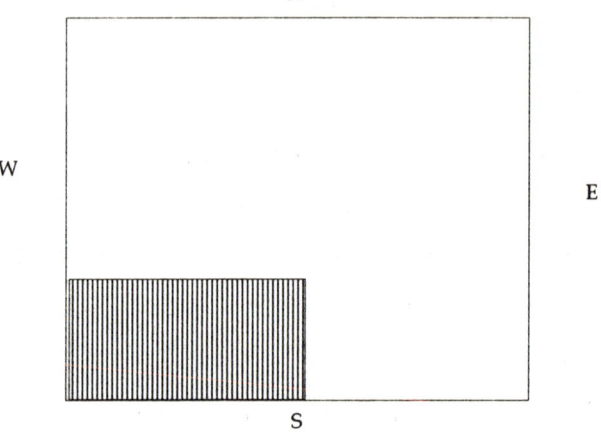

Main office in the south-west

3. The godown for raw materials should be situated in the south-west side of the building.
4. All waste products should be kept in the south-west side.
5. The electric gadgets, transformers, meters, etc, should be in the south-east side.
6. The watchman should be in the north-west corner.
7. Wells, fountains, underground storages, etc, should be in the north-east, north or east side of the plot.
8. The finished products of the factory should be stored in the south-west or west side of the building.
9. The workers' quarters should be in the north-west of the plot, far away from the office building or factory.

Landscaping

1. The south-west side of the garden should be dense with plants.

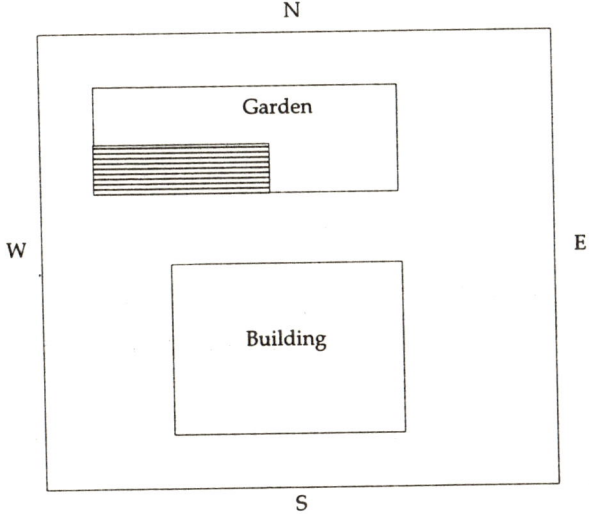

South-west of garden dense with plants

2. The garden should slope towards the north, east or north-east.

3. An underground tank or a pond should be in the north, east or north-east corner.

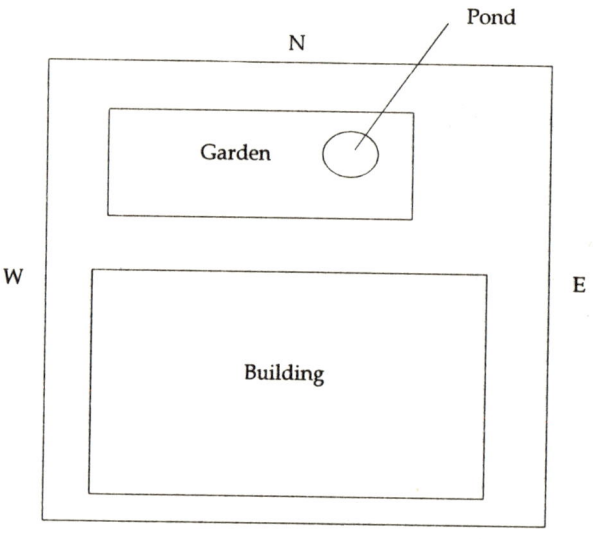

Location of plot in garden

4. Thick, massive walls in the south, south-west sides are a must, and they must be higher than the rest of the walls.
5. Electric gadgets for lighting the garden or fountain should be in the south-east corner.
6. Flowering and decorative small plants can be placed in the north, east, north-east or north-west.
7. A small cottage, where gardening implements can be stored, should be located in the south-west corner of the plot.

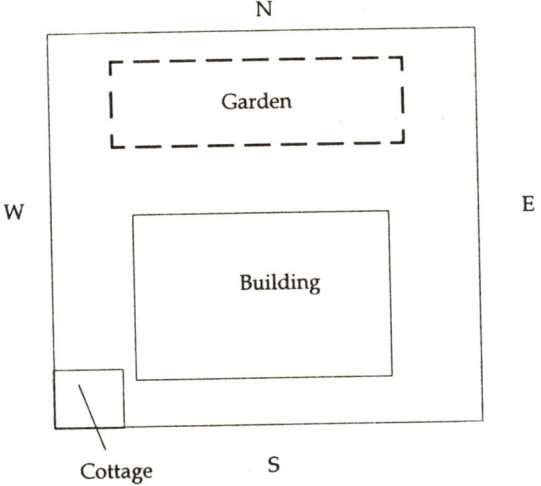

Cottage in the south-west

8. A few eucalyptus trees in the west side of the plot will prove beneficial.
9. Medicinal plants, herbs, aromatic bushes should be planted in the west side of the plot.

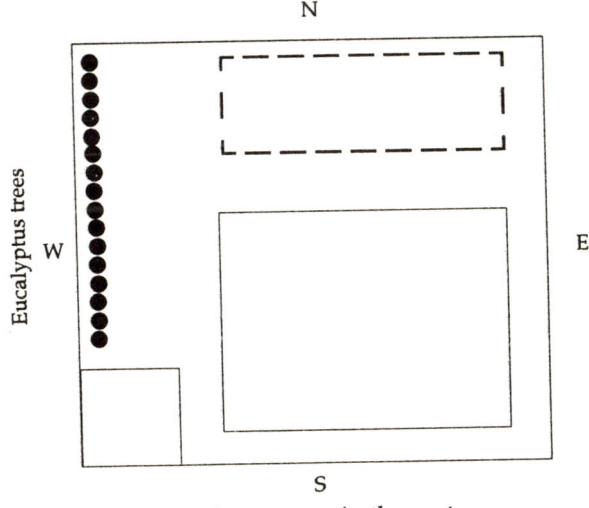

Eucalyptus trees in the west

10. A basil plant should be grown in the east, north-east, or north side of the house.
11. Tall trees should ideally be planted in the south-east or south-west side.
12. Medium-sized trees should be in the west or south.

Vaastushastra and Feng Shui

1. Feng Shui literally means 'wind' and 'water', respectively. Figuratively, it means the balance and harmony in the cosmic forces.
2. Vaastushastra deals with the five elements — earth, water, fire, wind and space. Feng Shui gives importance to fire, water, wood, gold and earth, with wind as the special attribute achievable by these elements.
3. Vaastushastra considers white and yellow soil good for construction, while Feng Shui stresses on a reddish or yellowish soil.
4. Vaastushastra considers a north-east directional flow of water conducive to fame and prosperity, while Feng Shui has no preferred water-flow direction, except that there should be a body of water in front of the main entrance of the house.
5. Vaastushastra stresses that windows should be located in the north, east or north-east sides, while

Feng Shui considers the north 'evil', and prefers windows in the south.

6. The kitchen, according to Vaastushastra, should be in the south-east corner, but Feng Shui has no such restrictions, except for the store which has to be in the south or east.
7. The north is considered as a door to spirituality according to Feng Shui. Vaastushastra dictates that it is governed by Kuber, the lord of wealth.
8. The north-east is a symbol of evil, so says Feng Shui. But in Vaastushastra, the direction is governed by Ish, the Lord Supreme.

Vaastushastra Remedial Measures

1. If the plot slopes from east to west, a relative raise or ascent towards the west should be provided in the landscaping at the planning stage.
2. Tall eucalyptus trees should be planted on the west side in the case of the plot sloping westwards.
3. In such a situation, the compound in the east should be built of a very light material.
4. Maximum number of windows should be provided on the east side.
5. If there is a well in the east or south-east side of the plot, it should be capped, for it may have disastrous results.

6. A slope in the plot towards the south, creating imbalance in the energy flow, can be offset by loading the south side with landscaping.
7. The compound wall should be thick and high in the south side.
8. Trees, like neem, should be planted on the south border.
9. A well in the south should be capped to avoid energy depletion.
10. If there is excess space in the west, a large number of eucalyptus trees can be planted.

Feng Shui Remedial Measures
1. Mirrors, representing a doubling of revenues, should be hung, especially in restaurants and offices.
2. An entrance with plants on either side of it brings prosperity.
3. Industrial ventures associated with uneven shapes should use plenty of lights to create balance and harmony.
4. Offices, homes, guest-houses, etc, should use chandeliers made of crystal for harmony and peace.
5. Fountains in the compound bring prosperity and wealth.

6. For career advancement, marital relationship and new business enterprises, wind chimes are recommended.
7. Colours denote and bring out certain characteristics in Feng shui. Here are some of them:

Red	—	Happiness, warmth and strength
Yellow	—	Power
Blue	—	Hope
White	—	Conducive environment, peace, happiness
Green	—	Growth
Orange	—	Happiness and power
Purple	—	Respect
Grey	—	Balance
Brown	—	Dullness and worry